WORK SIMPLIFICATION

AN ANALYST'S HANDBOOK

PIERRE THÉRIAULT

ENGINEERING & MANAGEMENT PRESS
Institute of Industrial Engineers
Norcross, Georgia, USA
http://www.iienet.org

01 00 99 98 97 96   6 5 4 3 2 1

Library of Congress Cataloging-in-Publication Data

Theriault, Pierre, 1932-
     Work simplification: an analyst's handbook / by Pierre Theriault.
          p. cm.
     Includes bibliographical references and index.
     ISBN 0-89806-163-6
     1. Reengineering (Management) 2. Methods engineering. I. Title
HD58.87.T48 1996   96-19351
658.4'063--dc20   CIP

Director of Publications: Cliff Cary
Book Acquisitions Administrator: Eric E. Torrey
Book Editor: Forsyth Alexander
Cover design: Marty Benoit

Engineering & Management Press
25 Technology Park
Norcross, GA 30092 USA
http://www.iienet.org
770-449-0461 phone
770-263-8532 fax

TABLE OF CONTENTS

FOREWORD

In today's tumultuous business and industrial world, faced with major changes on a planetary scale, managers can no longer manage as they did yesterday and hope to be in business tomorrow. Competition is now worldwide and markets no longer have borders. To become and remain competitive, companies must now, more than ever, increase their productivity.

Once intuition, flair, and past experience were sufficient to direct a project, launch a new product, or offer a new service. Today, managers realize that they need tools, methods, and systems capable of helping them do a better job, do more with less, make fewer mistakes, and succeed on the first try.

The concept of work simplification, or reengineering, provides managers with what they need to be as effective as they are efficient. Intuition, flair, knowledge, and experience need not be ignored; instead, they should be complemented with ways of doing things in a more systematic manner.

Work simplification offers managers an approach to problem identification and solution, one that formalizes work methods with a view to ensuring their effectiveness, improvement, and continuous updating. It also shows them how to prepare (or have prepared) the reference manuals and forms that are part of the data-gathering process so critical and necessary for making decisions and for the general well-being of the business.

Work simplification also covers the vital management activity of communication. It shows managers how to deal with their superiors, peers, and subordinates face-to-face, and how to conduct interviews that will be as useful to them as to their eventual interviewees.

Nothing must be left to chance. Success in the business world is rarely due to chance. Managers need a frame of reference, a group of methods and tools that will assure them that their actions are effective and their decisions pertinent. Work simplification offers such a frame of reference. It is a managerial responsibility to learn to use it.

Joseph Kélada
Professor-HEC, Université de Montréal

ACKNOWLEDGMENTS

My thanks go first to Dr. Ben Graham, Jr., for his unfailing support and encouragement in work simplification throughout the years and especially during the preparation of this book, which would not have been possible without his encouragement.

Thanks must also go to W. E. Hammer, Jr., for the many judicious comments and suggestions that made this book much better than it originally was.

Finally, I am grateful to Douglas M. Hird for his patience and friendship during the numerous years of our relationship. He undertook the formidable task of correcting the manuscript and offering suggestions that greatly improved its language.

INTRODUCTION

This guide focuses on administrative work simplification and process improvement with proven and easy-to-use methods.

While conducting different studies, analysts play a number of different roles, ranging from independent and self-sufficient experts to facilitators for a work group or team made up of both analysts and users. In this book, the term *analyst* is used to indicate the entire scope of roles. The discerning reader should note, however, that this author prefers the team approach for its immense productivity.

Analysts must adopt a study method with which they feel comfortable that, at the same time, their client can understand and approve without difficulty. Respecting the user's needs is a prerequisite for success. Also, despite the attention and care analysts may bring to the accomplishment of their mandates, they must always keep in mind that, in the development of new systems, creativity takes a large part. Not all methods can be reviewed in one guide; therefore, only those believed to offer the best possibilities for excellence are discussed.

Recommendations constitute the final part of all systems studies. It is therefore important to formulate them in a manner that ensures successful implementation. Graphic tools are particularly useful because they are easy to read and understand. They, along with oral and written communications, are covered in this book.

THE HISTORY OF
WORK SIMPLIFICATION

Xenophon (425-355 B.C.) is the first known work organizer. He studied shoemaking and the work of women in the home. In the Middle Ages and during the Renaissance, there were remarkable studies made of construction work such as the elevation of the obelisk at the Vatican. This operation, which mobilized 800 men and 140 horses, was broken down into 152 movements, each initiated by the sound of trumpets.

Under the reign of Louis XIV, Sébastien de Prestre, the Marquis de Vauban (1633-1707), timed landscaping projects and discovered a fundamental rule: supervision costs less than the reduction in productivity that results from no supervision.

In the eighteenth century, interest centered on division of work, expenditure of human energy, and quality and speed in the accomplishment of a task. Frederick Winslow Taylor (1856-1915) used these ideas at the end of the nineteenth century and the beginning of the twentieth, and the creation of scientific management is generally attributed to him.

Taylor's goal was increased industrial efficiency by increasing productivity and reducing costs. He believed that a salary increase would automatically result in an increase in productivity. He also maintained that the planning of tasks and their execution were to be kept separate.

Taylor was one of the first in the industrial era to measure and time the work of employees to find the best method of doing the work. This time and motion study (TMS) methodology approach to studying and understanding processes (manufacturing and business) continues to be built upon. His scientific management led to assembly lines used by Henry Ford and others in the automobile industry and subsequently in many other large production plants. TMS is still widely used today.

Taylor's hypothesis that increasing salaries would necessarily increase productivity was challenged by studies such as the Hawthorne experiment at Western Electric in the 1920s and those of industrial psychologists Mayo, MacGregor, and, more recently, Scott Myers and Frederick Herzberg.

The origins of the management principles practiced today are attributed to Henri Fayol (1841-1925). Unlike Taylor's scientific management, which is used only at the workers' level, Fayol's management principles may be applied to all levels of management and in any type of organization. Fayol's book *Administration industrielle et generale*, published in Paris in 1916, was translated and published as *General and Industrial Management* in New York in 1949. He was the first to identify the functions of management still used today:

- planning;
- organizing (which now includes coordination, which Fayol listed separately);
- directing (he used the word command); and
- controlling.

The influence of Fayol's book was immediately felt in the United States when it was published. Management consultants stopped thinking in terms of the worker at the bottom of the hierarchy and started looking at the entire company organization from top to bottom, just as Fayol had advocated.

Following Fayol's work and the advent of scientific management, a number of American engineers started to look at how to increase industrial productivity. Foremost among these pioneers were Frank Gilbreth, Allan Mogensen, and Ben Graham, all of whom sought a means of simplifying work so that it would be easier and still increase productivity. It was Mogensen who coined the term *work simplification*, now defined as the organized application of common sense to find better and easier ways of doing a job. Mogensen also directed his attention to office work. In the 1920s he created a two-week seminar entitled "The Management of Improvement" held each year in January in Georgia and New York.

Gilbreth is remembered for his pioneering work in the techniques of flow charting. Upon his death in 1924, his wife, Lillian, continued his work, concentrating on simplifying work in plants as well as offices.

She held conferences and seminars all around the world until her death in 1971 at the age of ninety-three. Today, there is a Gilbreth Medal awarded annually in England to the person who has contributed the most to the advancement of organization and methods, as work simplification is known in England.

Ben Graham, was a friend of both Gilbreth and Mogensen. He decided to tackle office work simplification only and created paperwork simplification. He was working for the Standard Register Company at the time. Graham died in 1960. His son, Ben, Jr., followed in his father's footsteps and conducts his seminars and conferences to this day.

These work simplification pioneers combined the fundamentals of motion study with a philosophy of eliminating waste. The significant difference between their approach and Taylor's was that they advocated the use of teams that allowed worker participation in the study of work simplification. Taylor excluded the worker on the basis that all planning and study of how the work was solely management's responsibility.

Following their footsteps, in the mid-twentieth century, W. Edwards Deming, who became an expert in the techniques of sampling, developed fourteen points for the improvement of quality, productivity, and competitive position. The first and fifth of these points were, respectively:

- to create constancy of purpose for the improvement of product and service; and
- to improve constantly and forever the system of production and service.

He also identified the "Seven Deadly Diseases" and a number of obstacles to improved quality.

Deming's approach is known as Total Quality Management, or TQM, so named by the Japanese. They believe that quality means:

- quality of work;
- quality of service;
- quality of information;
- quality of process;
- quality of division;
- quality of people, including workers, engineers, manager, and executives;
- quality of company; and
- quality of objectives.

Together, the Gilbreths, Mogensen, and Graham, Sr., created a large following in the field of work simplification, as did Deming. Graham, Jr., and Mogensen were among the founders of the

International Work Simplification Institute (IWSI) which, for many years, brought together thousands of professionals. Other American professional organizations that promote work simplification are the Institute of Industrial Engineers (IIE) and the Association for Systems Management (ASM). Internationally, in Québec, four people created the Institut des conseillers en organisation et méthodes (ICOM) in the early 1980s.

CONCLUSION

What started out long before this century as the organization of work became scientific management. It then became work simplification (known in Europe and in Canada as organization and methods) and encompassed quality circles in the 1970s and TQM in the early 1980s. It is now referred to as business process reengineering; however, it is all the same thing: namely, the organized application of common sense to find better and easier ways of doing a job.

This approach is more attuned to humans. Workers are not machines. They may slow or block the functioning of machines to show their dissatisfaction. It is therefore necessary to satisfy their needs and train them in a way that motivates them to do a good job and enjoy it.

This organizational method is constantly evolving. For example, women occupy a growing part of the work force. Lillian Gilbreth is a good example. As a psychologist and a mother of twelve, she was concerned with societal activities that needed modification in the areas of thought and behavior. That is why, today, management specialists and work simplification/business process improvement analysts are more interested in studying her work than that of her husband, who was a master of scientific management. It is possible that now, more than a century after the birth of this remarkable woman, a new revolution is necessary to render our thinking even more productive.

THE ROLE OF
WORK SIMPLIFICATION

Competition, market, and technological changes force companies to adjust and update their systems and methods. Although the organization of work should not have excessive influence, it is obvious that all company departments should be reviewed periodically, including those processes that cross departmental lines.

Before methods analysis can be explored, the role or mission of a *work simplification function* should be defined. One can define that role as follows: to advise the company on the best ways to use its human, physical, and information resources to improve efficiency and reduce costs. Like any other company function, the objectives of work simplification should be established before any action is taken.

Business process improvement/work simplification (BPI/WS) should not be limited to a single goal or activity; rather, it must focus on the whole organization. A senior manager responsible for BPI/WS should report to a high level executive such as the president and general manager or an executive vice-president. This is the best way to indicate the importance senior management has in a process improvement mission.

A CLEAR MANDATE

BPI/WS consultants must always think in terms of the company's welfare. They need a mandate that allows them to work along those lines, for they cannot conduct periodic business reviews without one. A typical mandate generally calls for:
- examining and reviewing all new procedures and methods,

forms, and systems before implementation;
- periodically reevaluating all existing systems and procedures;
- periodically reexamining all business processes and systems and questioning their goals, work methods, structure, equipment, personnel needs, and usefulness; and
- acting as a change agent within the organization.

The role of the mandate is to advise the company on the best ways to use its human, physical, and information resources. It is therefore important to define these resources, as well as what is meant by a *system*. *Human resources* are, obviously, the people needed to get the work done. Human resource processes should be well organized and work loads should be distributed properly. *Physical resources* are work methods, procedure manuals and forms, and office layouts, machines, and furniture.

BPI/WS analysts and consultants must ensure effective utilization of space and human resources through adequate management systems, proper training of the persons in the jobs, and structured departments with good work distribution.

Information resources are all useful data or documentation. They may be recorded on magnetic disks or electronic diskettes, printed on continuous or other paper, and entered on forms or included in financial and other reports. This also includes all employee knowledge and experience.

A system, then, is an organized collection of these physical and human elements. When they are taken into account, a clear mandate based on all the necessary components may be established. Specifically, these components are: methods, work flow, forms, space utilization, office equipment (machines and furniture), and procedure manuals. A clear mandate also includes the establishment of norms, work distribution, position descriptions, organization structure, and training (for the functioning of systems).

QUALITIES OF A GOOD BPI/WS ANALYST OR CONSULTANT

Usually, an analyst is primarily interested in systems while a consultant takes a more general approach to work simplification. In some organizations, both functions are linked; in others, they are distinct. Analysts are commonly called systems analysts. However, both analysts and BPI consultants need the same qualities to perform effectively, namely:

- a logical, analytical approach;
- intuition, ingenuity and imagination;
- good memory and sound judgment;
- tact and diplomacy;
- knowledge of office equipment, management principles, systems, and organizational study methodology; and
- a faculty for grasping the essential.

Two other characteristics are essential: a knack for invention and exceptional selling abilities. A good analyst or consultant must be particularly skilled at creation and innovation in order to design reforms after having studied actual situations. Analysts and consultants also must remember their intended roles and their functions within an organization. Their work and their behavior must be professional.

As for salesmanship, an analyst or consultant's product is an idea, something intangible, and thus is much harder to sell than a tangible product. It is therefore necessary to have a lot of patience, sincerity, and flexibility to succeed. For their products to be accepted and to make a contribution, they should anticipate objections and be able to refute them, one-by-one, with facts and not opinions. If an analysis is done in an objective and meticulous manner and the recommendations convey the best solution, logic will guide those who must make final decisions. It is a question of helping others understand an untenable position: any decision contrary to the recommendation should appear illogical.

THE CHANGING ROLES OF BPI/WS ANALYSTS AND CONSULTANTS

Years ago, in traditional, rigidly hierarchical organizations, direction flowed from above and was obeyed by each junior level. In such a setting, consultants were expected to dispense wisdom and pass judgment upon lesser mortals—a role not unlike that of a guru descending from the mountain top. Organizations have changed, and the role of analysts has changed with them. No longer are they expected to be the source of all wisdom. Instead, it is recognized that the knowledge necessary to bring about process improvement resides in the people who work day-to-day at the function being studied. Therefore, most studies are now done by a team.

Analysts or consultants are often called upon to act as leaders or facilitators of a process improvement team. It is, then, extremely important that an analyst or consultant be able to work with teams and team philosophies. A successful consultant or facilitator is always guided by this dictum: *the amount of process improvement is directly proportional to the involvement of the personnel regularly performing the function.*

In some cases an analyst may not even be the team leader, but rather another team member with special skills that can assist the other members in the research process. The consultant's critical role is that of a catalyst, teasing out information, welcoming questions and observations, and encouraging users to volunteer alternative solutions based on their practical experience in the area being studied. Consultants should assist them with the implementation of the team's recommendations.

CONCLUSION

With a clear mandate and an analyst or consultant that understands it, a business has a headstart on the path to process improvement. Another important step for the consultant is the study of business processes. That is the subject of the next chapter.

3

THE STUDY OF
BUSINESS PROCESSES

Private enterprises ensure their survival and growth by increasing their productivity. *Productivity* is a numerical comparison of output measured against overall resources used. *Production resources* include raw materials, machines, manpower, capital, and management.

It is possible to increase productivity by using better business processes. This can be done through work simplification, or an approach or methodology used to improve business systems. Work simplification offers effective methods for conducting business process studies as well.

Various means or techniques are used in a business process study. The work accomplished; the types of documents and printed forms used and their flow; the people doing the work; and when, where and how the work is done are all scrutinized.

Business systems studies should be done in all sectors of activity in private or public organizations, whatever their overall size. They also should be made on a continuing basis. If a business system is satisfactory, i.e., it meets the norms or the objectives, it may still be improved or replaced by a better system. If a business system is not satisfactory, i.e., it does not meet the norms or the objectives, it must be corrected or replaced.

Analysts and consultants should, first and foremost, direct their attention to unsatisfactory business processes so that they might be remedied. Attention then may be directed to satisfactory methods for improvement.

A BPI/WS analyst or consultant is the best person to lead business process studies. However, in any organization, the greater understanding management personnel have of the advantages of business process studies, the better the study results will be. The greater the number of people participating in the studies, the easier the implementation of new and/or improved systems will be. Studies made by groups or teams and led by an analyst or consultant are highly recommended.

Work simplification offers a very effective methodology for business process studies. This in turn helps with the implementation of BPI/WS. Once a business process study has been made, a company can concentrate on the methods necessary for improving its overall productivity.

THE FUNCTION OF ORGANIZATION

The organization or hierarchy of a company profoundly affects its productivity and processes, particularly in the United States. Understanding a company's internal structure is key in understanding its functions and designing a WS/BPI program that fits its needs.

In the business world, the word *organization* has several meanings. Linked with methods (as in organization and methods in Europe and Canada), it designates the people who manage all aspects of the company's structures and methods, including their creation, adaptation, retention, control, and improvement.

Organization is the way different company structures are created and relate to one another. It is also the way their functions are defined and their processes determined. Other processes establish the links between departments and the outside world.

The term is also used to clarify the relations between those who participate in the company's activities. Taken in this context, it is a way to determine the responsibilities and authority of those in different levels of the company; that is, responsibilities and authority relative to manpower, financial means, material, and machines, all of which are part of the company's resources.

It therefore follows that BPI/WS consultants must be familiar with how a company is organized without neglecting the informal organization, which the people of the company create amongst themselves.

THE LAWS OF ORGANIZATION

There are very few organizational laws for general applications, and those that do exist are not very clear. Believing that the laws of organization are based on mathematical and psychological research and that their application requires lots of experience, intelligence, knowledge, and ability are common errors. Most of the time, a good dose of common sense is all that is required. However, knowing the laws of organization may not be sufficient for effective application.

Most BPI/WS consultants spend about 99 percent of their time looking at methods and only about 1 percent looking at the structure of the company. This is unfortunate because time spent studying company organization usually generates greater savings of hours, days, and even weeks than studies of methods alone.

HOW ORGANIZATIONAL STRUCTURE CAN CAUSE LOW PRODUCTIVITY

The traditional methods for increasing productivity rarely succeed because they do not tackle a company's bureaucracy, which often is extensive. Yet, the reasons for low productivity usually can be found in a neglected organizational structure. Senior management often takes structures for granted, not believing they have anything to do with either plant or office productivity.

Most companies wait for serious problems to occur and then start looking at structures in a conventional manner. They redraw the organization chart, transfer some responsibilities from left to right, and fire a few workers at the low end of the hierarchy. This ignores the mission of each entity and the results each one should achieve.

HOW TO REVIEW COMPANY STRUCTURE

Management must carefully examine their structures, analyzing the number of management levels, the degree of managerial controls, and the cost of managing each employee. This can be done by disregarding the present organizational structure. Few organization charts are up-to-date. They only serve to communicate a structure and describe company bureaucracy without representing the strengths and weaknesses of the organization. Instead, the following questions should be asked: "if we were creating the company today, how would we organize it? How would we structure it?" In other words, those reviewing structures should not be influenced by what presently exists; rather, they should start from scratch.

Art Spinanger of Proctor and Gamble used to say that when faced with an existing system, one should ask: "If we eliminated it, stopped doing it, what would we miss?" This approach works with company structure as well.

EXERCISE

The president of ABC company asks for assistance in reorganizing and restructuring the company. He or she insists that, at the higher levels, there be no more than five administrators and that this number be the maximum number of subordinates as well.

He or she listed the company's activities as follows:

Accounting	Marketing
Accounts Payable	Office Services
Accounts Receivable	Personnel Admin.
Archives	Production
Billing	Publicity
Controller	Public Relations
Credit	Purchasing
Delivery	Recruiting
Human Resources	Research
Internal Audit	Sales
Legal	Sales Training
Maintenance	Word Processing
Management Training	Work Simplification
M.I.S.	

The challenge is to prepare the company's organization in accordance to the president's wishes. Figure 4.1 is one example of how such a chart could be prepared. It is not the only way, however. New functions or activities may be created, some may be eliminated, and others combined.

ORGANIZATION STUDIES

In organization studies, there must be a clear idea of what the company or the department is trying to do and what the results of their activities should be. In other words, what are their objectives?

THE DIFFERENCES BETWEEN COMPANIES

What type a company is determines how it is organized, although companies of the same type are not necessarily structured the same way.

President				
Vice-president level				
Marketing	Operations	Finance	Administration	M.I.S.
Managers level				
Marketing	Research	Controller	Office Services	BPI/Work Simplification
Publicity	Production	Credit	P.R.	Sys. Dev./ Programming
Sales		Accounting	H.R. Legal Internal Audit	Computer Ops. Archives (Records Mgmt.)
Assistant Managers level				
Sales	Delivery	Billing	Purchasing	
Training		A. Payable	Maintenance	
		A. Receivable	Recruitment	
			Mgmt. Training	
			Personnel Admin.	
			Word Processing	

FIGURE 4.1 - SAMPLE CHART FOR ABC COMPANY

The size of the company must be taken into account. The sole owner of a small company does most of the jobs: purchasing, sales, accounting, publicity, and planning. When the company grows, the need to be organized a little better is felt. What appears first is a need for specialization and an understanding of each person's responsibilities. In other words, who will do what?

The size of the company determines the kind of organization necessary for smooth operation. The larger the companies, the greater the need becomes for specialists and a well-structured organization.

THE CONCEPT OF SCOPE OF RESPONSIBILITIES

One of the general laws of organization addresses the scope of responsibilities. This law stipulates that one person cannot manage more than X number of employees at a time. The value of X varies. Some say it should be at least six, others maintain that it should be up to six (six being a limit). Actually, the number of subordinates depends on the experience of the supervisor and the tasks being done.

For example, a galley supervisor could manage a considerable number of slaves, as long as they were all doing the same thing. All that was required was for the whip to be long enough to reach each and every one of them when needed. And the job could be done without straining any mental capacities. On the other hand, the president of a multinational corporation composed of diversified companies should not try to be the general manager of each company. A president should not have to deal with all the middle managers on a daily basis. Serious problems would quickly result.

The law of scope of responsibilities influences company structures and imposes constraints on companies whose functions are complex. It is difficult to grasp a number of different concepts, particularly if circumstances call for moving rapidly from one to another. Under such conditions, it is imperative that a manager not have more than four to six subordinates. Levels of management also should be added, although not too many. The trend in the last decade has been to flatten organizations to a maximum of four management levels, e.g., president and/or chief executive officer, vice-president, manager, and supervisors.

THE CONCEPT OF AUTHORITY

There are two types of authority: line and staff. *Line authority* is a system under which the authority is exercised from top to bottom. It is as old as mankind and is the kind of structure Taylor suggested in scientific management. An obvious example is the armed forces of any country. The system is simple and logical. The problem, and it is a major one, is communication. It is difficult for orders to get all the way to the bottom or for messages to travel from the base up. The result is often all kinds of misinterpretation.

Line authority works more efficiently where there is delegation of authority. After defining their objectives, the persons responsible for a department or a team are left with a certain amount of autonomy regarding decisions and getting the job done. The higher the level of the manager, the more important it is to delegate authority.

Staff authority gives advice in a specialized field: personnel, legal, or accounting, for example. There is also a structure that combines the two. A line manager may have a specialist on staff to help make certain decisions.

Finally, companies may have links without any relation with authority (the informal organization). This is an important aspect of organizational life that an analyst or consultant must take into account.

A company should be organized on paper. Then, the personalities of those assuming the responsibilities need to be considered. A company is made up of a network of human relationships and interactions that often produce results sometimes very different from those expected.

CONCLUSION

Low productivity in companies has various causes but very often is the result of a faulty structure and the bad application of archaic principles. To increase productivity, senior management must accept that it is their responsibility to do so; it must be an objective of the entire senior management team.

Solving some problems of productivity begins when senior management decides to examine the company through its organizational structure, defining the company structure so that quality products and services are produced, at the lowest cost. Middle management should become responsible for the utilization of employees, while first level supervisors take on employee efficiency.

THE STEPS OF
WORK SIMPLIFICATION

Work simplification is a technique based on the analysis of the elements of a system or a procedure. The work simplification process may be accomplished in six steps. In this chapter, each step in the process will be examined in detail. Briefly, these are:

- selecting a situation;
- gathering all the facts;
- analyzing the facts;
- improvement;
- implementation; and
- follow up.

SELECTING A SITUATION

The first step in work simplification is the choice and definition of the system or process to be studied. A *system* is an organized collection of physical and human elements, while a *process* is a means used to produce certain results.

CHOICE

In most companies, there are plenty of systems and procedures. The question is, where to begin? The objective is to correct or improve systems and processes to increase productivity. Malfunctioning systems interfere with the objectives of the company. Therefore, it is logical to start where the most gains can be made or where the needs are the greatest.

A project imposed because of political considerations should be avoided. Instead, the analyst's skills should be used to identify the project. Such a rational analysis will ensure a better choice of project and improved planning.

The analyst should compile a list of possible studies/reviews (e.g., problems involving the production, unduly high costs, bottlenecks, time expended out of proportion, to results obtained, and others). It is not enough to examine unsatisfactory systems or situations that must be corrected or replaced; one must also consider satisfactory systems/situations where improvement is possible.

Determining criteria is next, i.e., on what basis will it be decided whether or not to look at a particular system/situation? Once systems or situations are selected, decide which has first priority, second, third, and so on, ranking the criteria and assigning each a numerical value.

In the list of projects, the systems and the processes are defined in very broad terms. Before starting the study, a clearer definition of the precise problem is necessary. This ensures that the study focuses on the real problem rather than pursuing a haphazard fishing trip over a broad and ill-defined area.

After each problem has been clearly defined, the objectives to be achieved by work simplification are identified, and the plans for the study/review are also prepared. To avoid confusion, errors, misunderstandings, and even disagreements, the following components of the study must be determined:
- the purpose of the study, its objectives and limits;
- the participating analyst or consultant's responsibilities;
- the timing (when) and the time (how long);
- the approach taken to make a success of the study; and
- the departments involved in the study.

In fact, the critical element at this stage is to establish clearly, with the persons interested or concerned, the exact nature of the study.

ESTABLISHING THE SCOPE OF THE STUDY

Once the nature of the study is clarified, the remaining task is to establish its scope. This includes:
- the number of employees affected;
- the kind of work done;
- the supervisors and manager(s) and their responsibilities,
- the manager to whom the person in charge of the study sector reports in terms of systems and departments; and
- where the study will start and end.

Problems may begin to arise at this point. Some people, when asked about their responsibilities, will look incredulous. This is symptomatic of an organizational problem: look at this particular problem first before examining business systems. As soon as the people and their responsibilities are identified, there ought to be a fairly clear picture of the area(s) that need the largest portions of study time.

A study may touch other departments that interact with that being studied, such as those supplying input and those receiving output. At the beginning, those departments may not be identified. It is necessary to investigate and verify a number of these relationships. When forecasting the study timetable, be sure to allow sufficient time for the activity.

MANDATES

There will be times when an analyst will not choose the system or procedure to be examined. Senior management or an immediate superior will make that selection. In other words, the mandate will be given. The first task, then, will be to clarify the mandate.

A clear mandate:

- helps determine precise objectives, helps establish a field of action, and helps the analyst make wise decisions;
- supplies a sound base for planning, full information, and a source of reference; and
- helps standardize methods.

It then becomes the analyst's task to define the boundaries of the system or procedure to be studied.

AUTHORIZATION

To study a certain system after it has been chosen and clarified, there must be authorization to start the work. How high in the organization should one go for this authorization? As high as necessary. It is better to go too high than not high enough.

It is often useful to discuss the project with the immediate superior of the department head whose area is being studied. At the same time, be sure to use the opportunity to solicit that person's point of view regarding the situation. Also ask about the department head's authority and responsibilities.

Then, meet the department head in question and explain the analyst or consultant role, as well as the mandate and why there is one. Proceed in the same manner even in cases where the mandate comes from the

department head. The objective is to find out:
- the department head's authority and responsibilities;
- the responsibilities and authority of the subordinates;
- what the problem is perceived to be; and
- the difficulties of the present situation.

Problems of organization are key at this point. For example, if the manager's point of view differs from that of the superior about the job, this misunderstanding absolutely must be settled before going any further. Any misconception should be discussed with the superior so that an understanding can be reached about the superior's expectations.

PLANNING

Good planning is the link between what one hopes to accomplish and the means at one's disposal. It determines the necessary steps, their interrelations, and their proper sequence. Its importance must never be underestimated, especially by those who believe they are so entrenched in the action that they have no time to think. In fact, if these people took time to plan, their output would probably increase considerably and they would not be constantly overwhelmed with work.

Planning consists of creating the activities necessary for accomplishing the objectives set out. It is based on the information acquired and the hypotheses developed. Facts are not sufficient; hypotheses based on the discovered facts are necessary, even though each hypothesis is only a supposition. The biggest error planners can make is to mistake their conjectures for the real thing. It is therefore important to remember on what hypotheses a strategic plan is based. Also, several hypotheses on the same subject should be generated. A project based entirely on a single hypothesis that turns out to be incorrect is likely to be abandoned quickly.

Planning often helps establish objectives. It has no meaning as an intellectual exercise if it does not aim at improving the quality of the work and making better use of available resources. It is particularly useful where resources are limited; it then serves to identify the priorities that guide resource allocations for maximum efficiency.

Every plan is different and fills a particular need. However, it is possible to state certain rules applicable to a majority of cases. A few of these general rules are discussed in the following paragraphs.

A plan must be simple and understandable. An unnecessarily complex plan leads to confusion, provokes resistance, and is not useful. Simple, concrete examples are also helpful.

A plan should meet the needs of its users in its format, presentation, vocabulary, and essence. It must be precise in its instructions; it should not be applicable in all cases.

A plan must be selective. The first function of a plan is to establish priorities. Even then, one should not ask a group of people to do a thousand things at once. It is preferable to prepare a well-established plan, even if it is not complete, rather than gather massive amounts of information that will overwhelm the users.

Those using the plan must be able to find its advantages. A plan must be designed so that advantages to using it may be recognized. The expected results must therefore be included as well as an action program. The plan can then stimulate the users and inspire them to accept the plan, and the planners will not have to defend constantly the need for a rational forecasting plan.

A plan must be flexible. Rarely are all of a plan's activities performed as originally forecasted.

A plan must be as flexible as the study for which it is intended. It should be possible to modify it and adapt it to new circumstances. It should never be considered an untouchable document, for as the situation gets clearer, elements will be added to it.

There are three main planning tools: the Gantt chart, the work timetable, and the critical path method.

◆   The Gantt Chart

While working for the U.S. War Department during World War I, Henry Gantt created a chart to control the production of war material. Named in his honor, this device is also sometimes referred to as a bar chart. Its function is to represent graphically the evolution of a project in comparison with its planned execution time. It is used to plan the time for a project's activities and to establish, in advance, each person's or each group's job in relation to the time variable.

Gantt charts are also used to control a project. One only has to enter the progress of the activities in relation to what was planned. The person responsible can see at a glance what is done and what is left to do. If controls are set at precise dates, they can be included as activities. With the use of codes or symbols, reasons for delays may be noted.

To compile a Gantt Chart, first draw a chart with the project's time scale (hours, days, weeks, and so forth) running from left to right on the horizontal axis. Next, on the vertical scale, enter the list of the project's activities in numerical sequence. The length of each activity or task is represented by a double horizontal line. The length of each line is proportional to the length of the activity. To show the task's progression, fill in the space between the double lines.

The Gantt chart has the following advantages:

- it is simple to set up and use;
- it does not require special training;
- it shows the evolution of the work;
- it indicates the entire program and its progress; and
- it combines both planning and control.

The main drawbacks are that it is not easy to see the relationships between activities, and it cannot show critical activities, upon which the length of the project depends.

Unless it is modified to the point of confusion, the Gantt chart will not indicate that task A must be finished before task B, or that a delay between tasks C and D is possible, though not necessary. In small projects, the person responsible must remember the links between tasks. For large projects, however, one cannot rely on memory, no matter how great, and this limits the value of the Gantt chart.

◆   The Work Timetable

A detailed *work timetable* (fig. 5.1), no doubt derived from the Gantt chart, regroups the main elements of a mandate onto a chart with the following headings:

- steps. This lists the activities needed to fulfill a mandate;
- done by. This is the name of the person(s) doing each task;
- calendar. In months, weeks, days, and hours, this is the timetable for the project; and
- hours. This is the number of hours allocated for each step of the project.

The time scale anticipated is indicated by two parallel lines, and the user darkens the space between these two lines to show which steps are completed and when.

◆   The Critical Path Method

The *critical path method* is a planning and programming system for complex projects that involve the simultaneous execution of numerous tasks, some or all of which may also interact with each other. This technique facilitates the accomplishment of the project with minimal cost or minimal time, or a combination of the two. It is based on the fact that usually only a small amount of tasks determines the time necessary

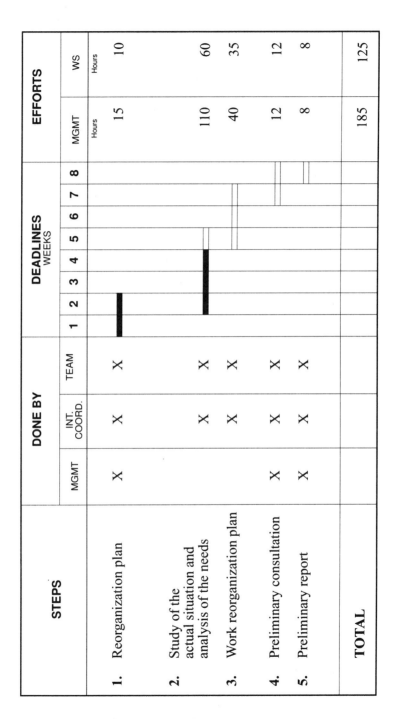

FIGURE 5.1 - WORK TIMETABLE (GANTT CHART)

to achieve a project. The longest sequence of those tasks constitutes the critical path; its length is that of the minimal execution time. The critical path principle is the basis for a number of techniques, the best-known of which is the program evaluation and review technique (PERT).

The path itself may be illustrated graphically by an arrow diagram. Each arrow represents a task, and the length of the arrow indicates the duration of that task. A digit on or under the arrow may also represent duration. When these arrows are combined, they form a grid network.

The entire network represents the logical interdependence between the tasks. It allows the visual highlighting of the task or job sequence, establishing the overall time span.

By centering efforts on the tasks in this critical path, it is possible to accelerate the execution of the entire project. For the tasks that are not on the critical path, there is a certain degree of freedom or margin of liberty that can optimize the allocation of material and human resources.

In order to use the critical path method efficiently, three questions must be asked before any task is undertaken:

- what tasks must be finished before beginning this one?

	A	B	C	D	E	F
A		✓			✓	
B						
C		✓				
D	✓					✓
E						
F	✓				✓	

FIGURE 5.2 - STEP ONE IN THE CRITICAL PATH METHOD

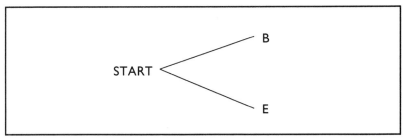

FIGURE 5.3 - TWO TASKS CONNECTED AT THE STARTING POINT

• what other task can be done concurrently?
• what comes after this task?

The following exercises and figures 5.2, 5.3, 5.4, 5.5, 5.6, and 5.7 demonstrate how the critical path method may be set up.

Plot a grid, on the upper line. Label all the activities: A, B, C, D, E, and F. Note the same activities in the left-hand column.

To start the activity in line A, must the activities in columns B, C, and so on be complete? If so, check off each one that must be done. Apply the same question for the activities in lines B, C, and so forth. See figure 5.2.

For this example, two lines remain blank: B and E. Therefore, those activities are the first to be done and can be done concurrently. In figure 5.3, a drawing of the two tasks connected at the starting point is used to separate these activities.

Plot another grid without activities B and E or use a colored pencil to cross them out.

Ask the same question for the remaining activities: to start the activity in line A, must the activities in columns C, D, and F be

	A	C	D	F
A				
C				
D	✓			✓
F	✓			

FIGURE 5.4 - PUTTING TASKS IN ORDER

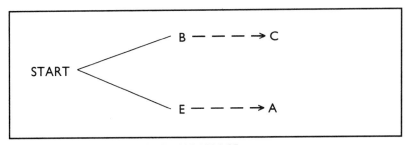

FIGURE 5.5 - PUTTING 'A' AND 'C' IN PLACE

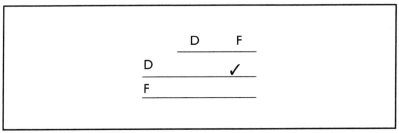

FIGURE 5.6 - A LAST CHECK AT ORDERING TASKS

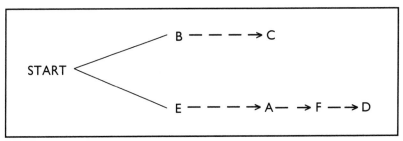

FIGURE 5.7 - FINAL EXAMPLE OF THE CRITICAL PATH METHOD

complete? See figure 5.4.

Lines A and C are now blank, as it was established in the first grid that A needed E before it could be done, and that C needed B. In the drawing created for activities B and E, put A after the E and C after B. They should be parallel to each other because they may also be done concurrently (fig. 5.5). Eliminate lines A and C, and question again. This time, line F remains blank (fig. 5.6). Put it beside A, so that D is at the end (fig. 5.7).

It was also established that D needed both A and F; thus it goes after F. The longest path is always the critical path. Therefore in this example, the sequence of the activities E, A, F, and D constitutes the critical path. Those activities determine the *global execution time*, i.e., adding the duration of each results in the total duration of the project. If efforts are focused on the activities of the critical path, the project as a whole will be achieved faster.

The CPM establishes the order of priority in which the activities must be carried out for the project to be completed in the shortest amount of time.

Regarding activities B and C, there is a certain degree of freedom in their completion. Therefore, the use of the equipment and the human resources can be optimized.

Activities		Minutes	Immediately preceding
A	Buy Food	45	
B	Peel Potatoes	10	
C	Trim Roast	05	
D	Cut Cabbage	10	
E	Make Sauce	10	
F	Make Gelatin	05	
G	Cook Cabbage	20	
H	Cook Roast and Potatoes	90	
I	Refrigerate Gelatin	30	
J	Eat the Main Course	25	
K	Eat the Dessert	15	

FIGURE 5.8 - TASKS INVOLVED IN CREATING A MEAL (EXAMPLE)

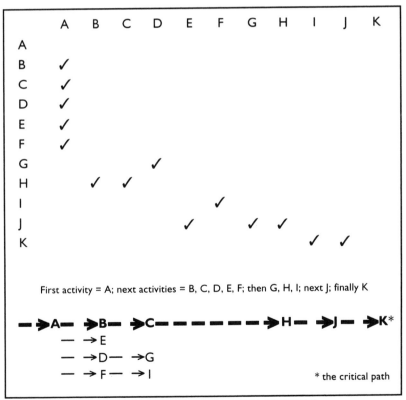

FIGURE 5.9 - STEPS TAKEN AND CRITICAL PATH (EXAMPLE)

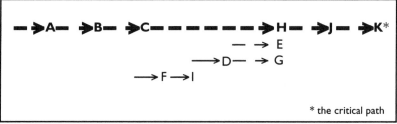

FIG. 5.10 - TASKS THAT CAN BE POSTPONED

◆   Example: Preparing for a Meal

The critical path method can help prepare a meal. The following meal must be prepared. The main course is a roast with sauce, cabbage, and potatoes. The dessert is fruit gelatin. List the tasks involved, assuming that:

- the food is not at hand;
- the sauce will be made separately; and
- the roast and the potatoes will be cooked together.

Figure 5.8 is an example of one possible list. The steps taken and the final critical path are illustrated in figure 5.9.

Since the meal is being prepared by one person, even if activities B, C, D, E, and F could be done concurrently, it is not possible for them to be done all at the same time. Using the critical path method, the cook can determine which tasks are critical and which may be postponed (figure 5.10).

Because the critical activities are A, B, C, H, J, and K, other activities may be arranged so that they are ready only when needed.

Either the Gantt chart, work timetable, or critical path method may be used to prepare for the review or study that has been chosen. Once it is planned, the next step is to gather the facts.

GATHERING THE FACTS

"A problem clearly expressed is already half resolved."
                              –C. H. Kepner and B. B. Tregoe

"If you can outline a problem, it can be resolved."
                                            –Edwin Land

In step two of work simplification, the analyst observes and registers all the facts pertinent to the study as it has been defined and elaborated.

The success of this approach depends on the quality of fact gathering. These facts serve as a basis for the third step, namely, critical examination and analysis.

THE INTERVIEW
An interview is the fundamental technique for acquiring all the information necessary for problem-solving. It also allows the analyst's ideas for improving the situation to be accepted. However, interviews demand a highly developed set of skills and should be conducted only by experienced analysts.

Different interviews breed different kinds of questions. Figure 5.11 summarizes the typical questions to ask.

◆   Preparation
The interview preparation varies according to the subject's position in the organization's hierarchy. However, no matter who is being interviewed, the objective(s) of the interview must be defined. Is the point of the interview to get information, to communicate information, or to influence?

Gathering information about interviewees and their work, logically preparing and grouping key questions, and sending the interviewees a list of questions that need research or calculations are all part of the preparation process.

An appointment must be made with the subject, preferably at his or her place of work. If the latter is not possible, for political or physical reasons, choose a place where there will be few interruptions and the atmosphere will be relaxed. It is also important to leave it to the interviewee, as much as possible, to choose the time, so that his or her work day is not overly disturbed.

Generally, morning interviews work best. The advantages are:
- they allow the analyst to complete notes the same day;
- they allow the analyst to draw up a flow chart the same day;
- the employees are fresh, fit, and free from concentration, as is the analyst; and
- the employees have not yet faced the problems of the day.

One must also determine the length of the interview. Interviewees will feel reassured from knowing that there is an end in sight. It follows that the analyst should be on time and should not prolong the interview without the subject's approval.

Moreover, it is difficult to remain on a subject beyond a certain

Types	Objectives	Examples
According to facts	Obtain information Open the discussion	Who? What? Where? How?
Explanations	Obtain motives and explanations Broaden the discussion Develop additional information	How can we resolve this problem? What should we take into consideration? How to . . . best?
Lead, train	Introduce new ideas Submit a suggestion	Should we consider this point, this way? Would it be possible to . . . ?
Choice hypothesis	Develop new approaches Suggest another acceptable opinion Modify the discussion	Let's suppose this way of doing: what are the implications? Is the way of doing it somewhere else applicable here?
Alternative	Choose between two or more alternatives to reach agreement	Which one would be best? A or B?
Coordinate	Give approval to prepare the way for implementation	Can we agree that this is the next step? Do we have general agreement for this action plan?

FIGURE 5.11 - TYPICAL QUESTIONS ACCORDING TO TYPE OF INTERVIEW AND OBJECTIVE.

length of time. It becomes necessary to stop in order to assimilate the information obtained. This is why it is preferable to end at the established time, even if it necessitates an additional meeting at a later time.

A flexible attitude is best; one should avoid over-preparation and prejudice.

Taking notes during an interview is useful, if not indispensable. It is usually ill-advised to rely on memory alone, for the information the interviewee will offer is too important to risk its loss. It should be noted that, if taking notes prolongs an interview somewhat, subsequent interviews will most likely be shorter.

There are two main interview approaches. One is based on the objective and the other is based on the subject's hierarchical level.

◆   Objective-Based Interview

There are three stages in an objective-based interview, and an analyst should take notes during each. The stage at which the analyst is in his or her study will influence his or her objective during the interview. Ideally, each of these stages should be a separate interview, but time often forces analysts to combine all three objectives during a single interview. The introductory interview is replaced by an introduction, the in-depth interview by the main part of the interview, and the clarification interview by a conclusion.

The introductory portion or introduction interview allows the subject and interviewer to become acquainted. The goals at this stage are: for the subject to recognize the analyst's competence, to encourage the subject to be open, and to prepare to develop plans from the information obtained. During this process, the analyst's notes should be brief. They are used for gathering more detailed information during the in-depth interview.

The main stage or in-depth interview portion is critical. At this point the analyst encourages the subject to provide as much information as his or her position allows about the procedure or system under study. Subjects are asked to describe their work, to examine obscure details, and to understand the flow of the data. The analyst should try to summarize the information obtained to eliminate all misunderstandings and to reaffirm the interviewee's trust. During the in-depth stage, detailed notes should be taken. They should produce a more precise view of the procedure or system being studied.

The clarification stage or conclusion interview should bridge gaps, evaluate new ideas, recognize the interviewee's contribution, ensure future collaboration, and encourage the acceptance of changes. The analyst's notes should again be brief, because, at this stage, he or she is only clarifying certain points.

◆ Level Interview

Analysts do not seek similar information from senior management, middle management (operations managers), or operations personnel, nor do they use the same kind of language for interviews with each.

For example, senior management should be asked to discuss objectives and policies in a broad sense. From middle management should come clarifications of the policies, and operations personnel should supply details about the actual tasks they perform.

Avoid using technical terms with senior management; with middle management, some may be used, but in moderation. Operations personnel will expect a number, however.

How one communicates competence also will vary. With senior management, an analyst must demonstrate his or her capability of carrying out the study. For middle management, such knowledge need only be demonstrated if and when necessary. With the doers, a professional image is necessary, but not to the point of irritating them.

An interviewer must empathize with the interviewee's place from the very first meeting. Very often, the interviewee considers the analyst a troublemaker. At a time when the subject's energies are directed toward solving his or her own problems, an analyst may be seen as a third party whose influence (probably negative) must be guarded against. In the first place, he or she does not believe that someone else can solve his or her particular problems. Who knows the situation better? All that is necessary, he or she feels, is a few more employees to do the work and a month or two to get up-to-date. It is therefore necessary to address an interviewee with tact.

It may happen, that in a climate of trust during an interview, an analyst will receive confidential comments from employees touching on personal problems. The analyst should, tactfully, invite such employees to talk to their immediate superior. If, however, the situation turns out to be general, this kind of problem should be discussed with the BPI/WS department head. The possibility of an intervention at another (higher) level can then be evaluated.

◆ **Introducing the Analyst**

The manner in which an analyst is introduced is important. Ideally, the subject's supervisor or manager should introduce the analyst and explain, in a few words, the analyst's presence.

Whether introduced by the employee's supervisor or by themselves, analysts and consultants must remember that they are there to learn something and greatly need the help of those being met. It is the interviewer's responsibility to ensure that a good working relationship is established for the free exchange of ideas and information.

An interviewee must be convinced of three things:

- the analyst is not there to turn everything upside down but to improve the situation, if possible;
- the analyst has the experience and knowledge that can be used to improve work; and
- the person being interviewed can contribute his or her own ideas and knowledge to change things for the better.

◆ **Listening**

The best way to discover what the interviewees have to say is to listen to them. This means paying attention to what is being said. It is not enough for the other party to talk without interruption. The analyst conducting the interview must also show that he or she understands what is being said and that it makes sense.

Even silence can incite talk. Sometimes subjects will stop their conversational flow because they expect the interviewer to say something or because they want the interviewer's comments. Silence in such circumstances should encourage the interviewee to continue. Often, this is the point when the interviewer will learn things that are likely to be most useful for the study.

There are other ways to restart the flow of talk. One is to repeat the interviewee's last sentence. Another is to summarize what has just been said in the most objective manner possible.

A recap that retains the main idea indicates that the employee's opinions are considered important. Moreover, it gives him or her time to reformulate particular thoughts and add other details that might not be easily or fully understood. Thus, the interviewer is more apt to grasp what the person being interviewed really wanted to say.

In his book, *Management Principles and Technique*, Pierre Contant provided the following example as an effective approach:

Interviewee: "We have been doing this work this way for years. We have always had difficulties doing it. We never balance out at the end of the month and it is always our fault."

Interviewer: "You feel that the work could be done another way."

Throughout the interview, an analyst must keep in mind that those being interviewed have banks of useful knowledge they do not realize they have. They may, and probably will, contribute many practical ideas that the interviewer would never discover on his or her own.

A successful interview is indicated by an exchange of useful information and points of view. Only a modest and likable attitude, and, by the same token, a courteous one, will allow this highly successful and fruitful exchange to occur.

The effective analyst believes that every contact with clients is an occasion to promote work simplification.

For shareholders and managers, increased productivity and profits necessarily come from removing the barriers to their growth. Workers are interested in seeing growth in the company for which they work, and their salaries and promotions depend on it. Analysts should remind their contacts repeatedly that the goal of BPI/WS is to reach these legitimate objectives.

Another method of gleaning additional information is for the analyst to act as if he or she knows very little or even nothing at all about this subject. Actually, this probably will not be much of an act, for if the interviewer had full knowledge of the facts, there would be no need for the interview. Once the interviewer has established a climate of confidence, the employee is happy to explain what goes on.

The interviewer should ask how the interviewee would resolve the problem. To make sure that he or she is not imposing ideas, the interviewer should encourage the subject to put forward all possible solutions. Each can then be examined in turn.

In this fashion, it is entirely possible that those interviewed will find the solution to the problem themselves. They then will be that much more inclined to implement it because it will be their solution.

It is important that the analyst give credit where credit is due. All contributions must be recognized and relayed to the appropriate supervisors.

◆ Controlling the Interview

Allowing the interviewees to express themselves is important; however, the interview must also stay on track and accomplish the tasks it set out to accomplish. One way to reach this goal is to build upon information already acquired. The interviewer selects and repeats certain words to indicate a need for expansion on the subject.

An interviewer should control the interview and should not move too quickly through the process. Ask one question at a time and vary each according to the interviewee's rhythm. As much as possible, avoid terms that are too technical, abstract, or emotionally charged.

Taking notes is another means of controlling an interview. While those being interviewed give a general overview of their operating methods, take only a few notes. This allows them to become accustomed to the note-taking process and provides highlights for reorienting the interview later, if necessary.

At the in-depth stage, notes need to be more comprehensive. The analyst needs as complete a picture as possible, without zeroing in on what goes well and what does not or to any particular way of doing things. A question mark may be placed next to the points that will need to be clarified later. During this interview or stage, if the subject mentions a document, book, or register, ask to see it. Carefully note the title, the number, and a description of each for later identification. Otherwise, try to refrain from interrupting.

The concluding interview or clarification stage is where notes are most useful for controlling the interview. Using the notes taken in the in-depth stage, the analyst states his or her understanding of the explanations. The analyst should ask all the questions that came to mind while the interviewee spoke during the in-depth period.

It is also the time to examine, in detail, all the documents the interviewee mentioned. Blank forms and documents are not helpful; it is the nature of the information entered on these forms that is crucial. From whom and whence does the information come? What does the interviewee do with it and where does it go from here?

◆ Interview Pitfalls

There are pitfalls to avoid during an interview. For example, try not to make small talk. Some analysts err in believing that idle conversation will help the person being interviewed relax. This is not true. A direct approach is best. Hesitating to broach the subject may make a bad impression.

On the other hand, an analyst should not transform an interview into an interrogation session. Firing off a line of direct questions point blank will probably make the interviewee nervous; asking too many leading questions will make the problem even worse. Moreover, interviewees often try to formulate an answer they think the interviewer wants to hear. It is therefore better to let the conversation flow as freely as possible. This allows the interviewees to express what is important to them.

It is, of course, necessary to ask questions, but, in general, it is best to avoid "yes or no" questions. Beware also of questions that produce answers such as "often" or "sometimes."

Another pitfall to avoid is expressing opinions. This includes gestures, voice intonations, and facial expressions that indicate feelings.

An interviewer must not put anyone on the defensive by criticizing how things are being done. Even if the criticism is not interpreted as a direct attack, it would probably prevent a future discussion from being devoid of prejudice.

The analyst must also be careful not to overpraise. Interviewees may use such an attitude to deduce that their solution is the best one and even strongly oppose any other solution.

The analyst should never raise a point diametrically opposed to that of the interviewee. An interview that becomes an argument will not garner proper results.

POST-INTERVIEW

To conclude the interview, the analyst should recapitulate the main points raised during the interview, thank the subject for his or her cooperation, leaving the door open for a subsequent interview in case supplementary information becomes necessary.

As soon as possible after the interview, the analyst should put the interview notes in order, completing them while the conversation is still fresh in his or her memory. This is the time to separate facts from opinions and deductions, evaluating the importance and meaning of the facts. They should be filed in a logical order by function, administrative unit, or whatever is most sensible. The analyst will also start to formulate conclusions and measure their scope.

Now is the time to reexamine the interview's objectives. Have they been reached? Is additional information needed? What was the impact of the interview on those interviewed? Did their attitude remain positive? How would they react to changes? And one final question: what could have made it a better interview?

Upon gathering the facts from interviews, the analyst should focus on recording them as clearly, precisely, concisely, and completely as possible.

COMMON TECHNIQUES FOR RECORDING FACTS

The three most common techniques for documenting facts are: the narrative technique, the graphic technique, and the chart technique.

The *narrative technique* is a simple, written description of facts as they present themselves. This method has the advantage of simplicity. Nothing need be learned to accomplish it. On the other hand, it has its disadvantages. It is time-consuming, does not always present a clear, precise, concise, and complete record, and does not lend itself easily to analysis.

The *graphic technique* uses symbols and codes. Often, one can summarize a complete process in a single page that is easy-to-read and understand. The disadvantage lies in the user's having to learn a new language: the meaning of graphic symbols.

The *chart technique* involves putting the starting elements of the facts, or the *interveners*, on the horizontal axis. This is the source document of an activity, department, or person concerned. The base of each activity is plotted on the vertical axis. Under each column, one enters the steps and interventions in a narrative form. This technique is simple to prepare and use, it does not necessitate special training, and it is easy to read and understand. It is most suited for administrative, repetitive, and structured tasks; it may become confusing if it is not prepared correctly or is used improperly. Figure 5.12 includes examples of different charts that may be used to record facts.

Over the years a number of powerful tools (other than the chart techniques discussed earlier) have been developed for recording and analyzing the data used in work simplification. Some of these tools or documents are covered in detail in the sections that follow.

Traditionally, analysts have used preprinted forms and completed them with pen or pencil. Today's researchers should be aware, however, that these forms are available (or can be easily created) with computer software. Moreover, for accuracy and speed, especially in correcting charting errors, computer software is unparalleled. A professional analyst must master computer technology in this area.

Many different software packages exist. They range from the highly specialized, which are developed specifically for analysis, to the more general, which can be applied to a wide variety of charting situations. An example of the former is the package produced by the Ben Graham Corporation for procedure flow charts.

More general products include CorelDraw!, PowerPoint, and CorelFlow! (designed strictly for flowcharting). Mastering one or more

Name	Description	Other Name
Paperwork flow chart	Gives an overall view of the circulation of documents	Flow chart
System flow chart	Gives a general view of a set of procedures	Systems analysis chart
Flow diagram	Shows the path of movement of documents, objects, or activities of the workforce	Circulation diagram, Layout flow chart, Flow diagram, Process layout
Work distribution chart	Shows the distribution of work in a process	
Procedure flow chart	Shows the activities of a procedure in order	Multi-column flow chart
Flow process chart	Sets in order and shows graphically the different phases intervening in an execution process	Process analysis chart

FIGURE 5.12 - EXAMPLES OF CHARTS FOR RECORDING THE FACTS

Symbol	Activity	Description
○	Operation (handling or adding to)	An operation takes place: 1. A characteristic of an object or document is modified; the document is divided or linked with others; it is prepared for another operation (movement control or filing); 2. A person performs specified tasks, receives or gives information, makes a calculation or plans.
□	Control (inspection/ checking)	A control takes place: 1. An object/document is examined for identification or its characteristics are checked for quality/quantity. 2. A person does one of the above tasks.
D	Delay (or filing)	A delay happens when an object, document or person remains inactive between two operations.
⇨	Transport (movement)	Indicates an object or document changing hands or location. A movement that is part of the operation or made by the same person at his workplace during operation or control is not considered a "movement."
▽	Filing	Filing occurs when a document is placed in a particular order in a location provided for the purpose.
△	Stocking (archives)	Stocking occurs when an object is placed in a particular place for conservation; ie., to protect it from any unintended movement.

FIGURE 5.13 - SYMBOLS FOR PAPERWORK FLOW CHART

of these allows an analyst to replicate all the traditional work simplification tools in electronic form.

◆   Paperwork Flow Chart

Flow charts help in the logical analysis of the elements of a system/ procedure. A *paperwork flow chart* shows the step-by-step realization of an activity. Its objective is to represent, in correct order, the different phases in the execution of a procedure and the flow of its documents.

Each symbol on the chart has a precise interpretation. These are shown in figure 5.13.

◆   Exercise

The following exercise shows how the actions involved in transcribing a letter might be recorded on a flow chart.

A stenographer sits at a desk. He or she collects a steno pad and a pencil, stands up, and walks to an executive office about twenty feet away. He or she takes dictation of a letter and returns to the desk. He or she selects and arranges paper and carbon paper and inserts them in a typewriter. He or she types the letter, removes it from the typewriter, and extracts the carbon paper. He or she reviews the letter for errors, enters it in the signature register, and returns to the executive office with the signature register. The executive proofreads the letter and signs it. The stenographer returns to the desk and types the address on an envelope into which he or she inserts the original of the letter. The envelope goes in an "out" basket, and the stenographer files the copy in the "correspondence" file for the day.

The flow chart for this process might look like that in figure 5.14.

◆   Flow Diagram

A *flow diagram* (fig. 5.15) is the representation in space of a process or a procedure's activities. It is also a picture of the space where the process or the procedure is taking place. The objective of a flow diagram is to place physically the activities linked to one or more processes or procedures.

By showing the relations between activities and space, the flow diagram can reveal poor equipment or space utilization, an irrational flow of work, complicated routing, documents or people going back and forth, or even poor allocation of space.

No form exists for this exercise. One simply draws a plan of the premises and indicates everything that can have an influence on the

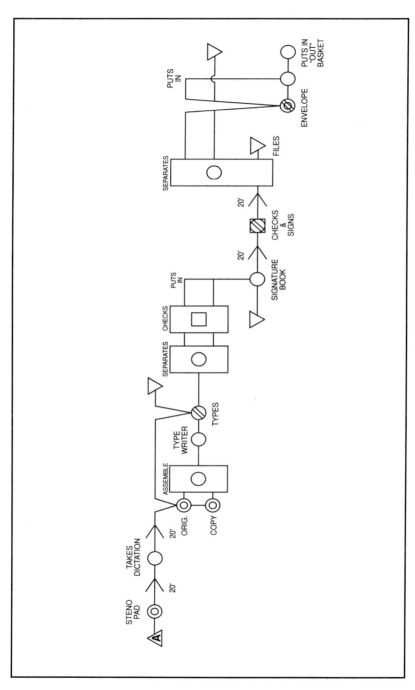

FIGURE 5.14 - FLOW CHART EXERCISE:
"LETTER TRANSCRIBED BY A STENO-TYPIST"

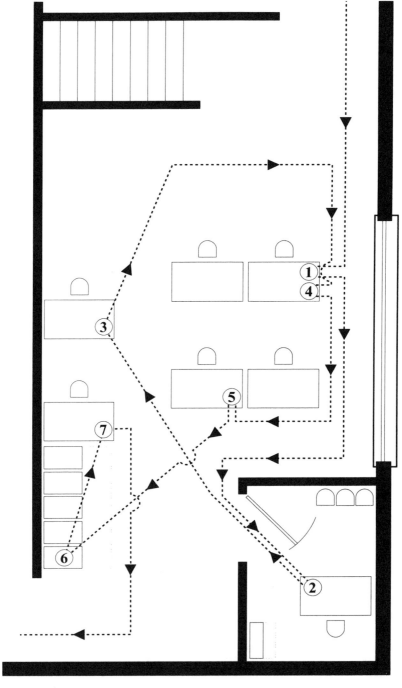

FIGURE 5.15 - FLOW DIAGRAM EXAMPLE

allocation of space. It is preferable to make a plan layout to scale, using one-fourth of an inch per foot or one centimeter for every four centimeters.

Lines and arrows may be used to indicate the flow of documents and/or people in the sector where the processes or the procedures are taking place.

◆   Work Distribution Chart

A *work distribution chart* is used to gain an overall view of the work being done in a department or in a single, well-defined unit. This helps consultants analyze the distribution of work.

The chart includes a description of each group member's tasks as well as the time allocated to each task in relation to the group's functions or activities.

By showing in a logical and orderly fashion who does what and how much time it takes, the work distribution chart may be used for two purposes: analysis and cost establishment.

For analysis, it demonstrates:

• the time used for various tasks and functions;
• the use of each worker's experience and knowledge;
• the links between the worker's tasks and the group's functions;
• the distribution and the division of work within the department or unit; and
• the management of the worker's efforts as they relate to the organization's functions.

For cost establishment, the table may be used to determine the average cost of each task and activity, as well as the total cost.

The work distribution chart (fig. 5.16) is a text-based entity and consequently does not have a special form or symbols.

◆   Procedure Flow Chart

The *procedure flow chart* represents a sequence of administrative operations that aim for the same results or fulfill the same function. These operations may be occurring at one or more work stations in a department or in several different departments. It supplies detailed information in correct sequence, on everything related to a procedure: the organizational elements, personnel, activities, work place, office equipment, forms, reports, registers, and more.

To produce a procedure flow chart, there are several rules to follow:

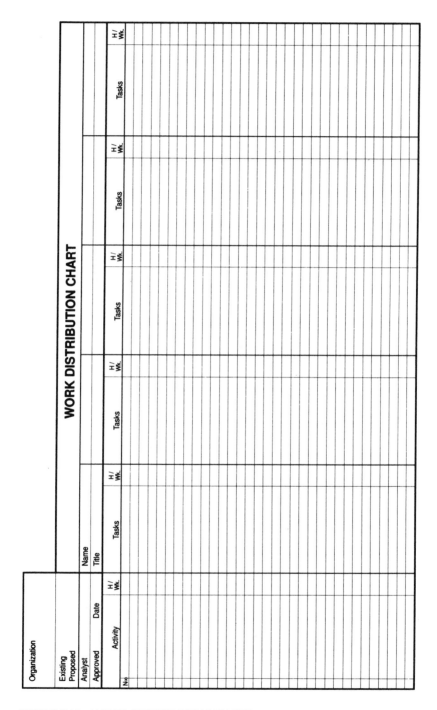

FIGURE 5.16 - WORK DISTRIBUTION CHART

- draw horizontal lines to separate the various parts of the company included in the study;
- use as many lines as necessary for the company's departments;
- each symbol should have a definition;
- if necessary, the execution time and the distances should be noted near the symbols;
- the arrow for the transport symbol should always point in the direction of company's departmental movement;
- the means of transport should also be noted;
- except for the symbols for adding information and checking, two symbols should not appear on the same vertical line;
- no line of a flow chart should appear without a symbol; and
- identify the flow chart completely: give the procedure title, the analyst's name, the date, and the name of the department or section studied.

◆ Exercises

The first exercise creates a procedural flow chart for an accounts payable clerk.

Roger is a conscientious clerk in charge of all the payments in his department. These are the main elements of his job:

Roger picks up an invoice (F.1234) in his in-basket and examines it. After making sure that it is meant for his department, he stamps the back of the invoice "received" and initials it. He also writes the date it was received on the reverse side of the invoice and records the invoice in his accounting register, initialing the entry. He then prepares a check requisition for the accounting department by typing F.2468 in triplicate. He signs the requisition and sends the original to accounting. He staples the invoice to the first copy, which he files in the file for the supplier awaiting the check. The last copy goes in a pending file.

Describe Roger's job with a flow chart. (One result is illustrated in figure 5.17.)

The next exercise shows how a procedural flow chart may be prepared for a bill payment process.

At the end of each month, Pauline worries about the number of bills she has to pay. She sits at her desk, pulls out her checkbook and pen and prepares to pay the month's bills. The envelopes are piled on her desk, and the stamps are in the top right-hand drawer. Pauline takes an envelope, opens it, and removes the bill and a return envelope. She

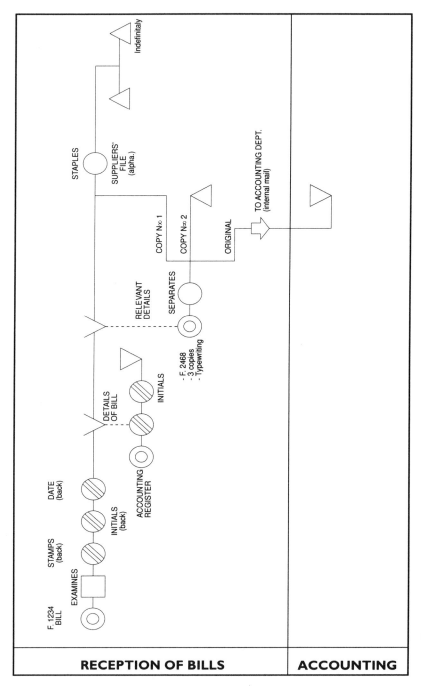

FIGURE 5.17 - PAPERWORK FLOW CHART
"ACCOUNTS PAYABLE" EXAMPLE

throws the opened envelope in the waste basket. She examines the bill to make sure there are no errors. Sometimes she asks herself why she has made such an expenditure, but, usually, she pays the bill anyway. She writes a check, separates the tear-off and return portion from the bill, enters the number and the date of her check, and files it alphabetically in an expenses file for an indefinite period. She puts the check and the return portion in the pre-addressed envelope, seals it, affixes a stamp, and places it on her desk. She repeats the operation until all the bills have been paid. Finally, she asks her son to put them in the mail box on the corner of her street.

The flow chart for this procedure may resemble that in figure 5.18.

CRITICAL ANALYSIS AND EXAMINATION OF POSSIBLE SOLUTIONS

The objectives of the third step of work simplification are:

- to question systematically each element of a procedure; and
- to propose various solutions to improve or correct a system or procedure.

For a critical examination of the facts, an analyst should maintain a questioning attitude and first asking, "can we eliminate it, stop doing it?" For each job activity, the following questions should be asked:

- What is the object or goal of this activity?
- Where or in what place is it being done?
- In what sequence or at what time is it being done?
- Who does this activity?
- How is it being done or what method is being used?

Also keep in mind Peter Drucker's question: "What is the point of doing at the lowest cost what should not be done in the first place?"

In short, these questions are: what, where, when, who, and how. After each of these questions add another: why? Where, when, and who allow change, combination, and rearrangement. How allows improvement or simplification. Why eliminates the unnecessary. These are illustrated in figure 5.19.

To generate solutions, one must adopt a creative attitude. For each work activity, ask the following questions:

- What else can we do? Why?
- Where else can we do it ? Why?
- When can we do it? Why?
- Who could do it? Why?
- How best can it be done? Why?

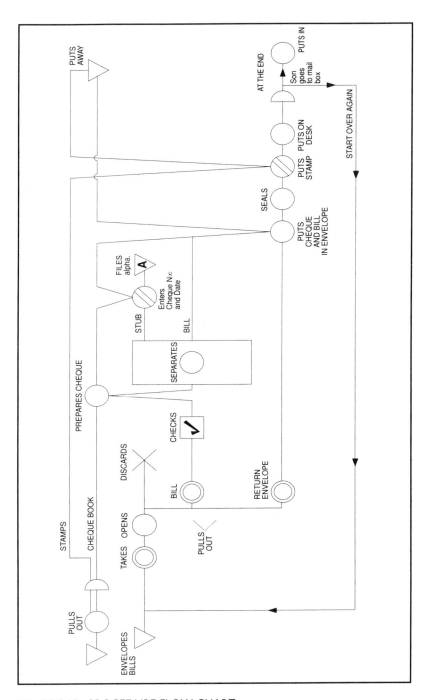

FIGURE 5.18 - PROCEDURE FLOW CHART
"PAULINE PAYS HER BILLS" EXAMPLE

ACTIVITY EXAMINED

	Critical examination		Possible solutions	Solution chosen
What	What is being done?	Why is it being done?	What else can be done?	What will we do?
How	How is it being done?	Why this way?	How?	How?
Who	Who does it?	Why this person?	Who else could do it?	Who will do it?
When	When is it done?	Why then?	When?	When?
Where	Where is it being done?	Why there?	Where else?	Where will it be done?

FIGURE 5.19 - CRITICAL ANALYSIS AND EXAMINATION
OF POSSIBLE SOLUTIONS

When examining possible solutions, the analyst is faced with two basic options. First, it is possible to seek solutions independently. This is the more frustrating and difficult of the two. Data will not be forthcoming, participants will assume that the analyst is already aware of key information, and there will be solid resistance when the time comes for implementing the chosen solution(s).

The other option is adopting a team approach. If, by acting as a catalyst, one encourages and ensures the participation of the people involved, the following results can be expected:

- resistance to the proposed change will diminish or disappear;
- those involved will get more satisfaction from their work; and
- the number and the quality of the proposed solutions will increase.

In short, for the critical examination as well as for the generation of solutions, the involvement of those doing the work can produce the most interesting ideas for solving a problem. Team discussions often turn out to be more profitable than a simple consultation. An analyst acting alone can hardly find answers to all the questions that must be asked. This is particularly true of the "why" questions. In many instances, it is the people directly involved, the worker or the supervisor, who can best supply the answers. At times the analyst must also ask other departments, such as quality control, purchasing, or sales. As a matter of fact, making a critical examination of each activity of a system or procedure without consulting those actually doing the job is asking for resistance when the time comes to implement a new system or procedure.

PRIORITY

In principle, each activity must be examined. Clearly, however, not all activities have the same importance. An order of priority should be established.

Basically, there are two types of activities:

- the main activity, which influences all or many of the others, and if it is eliminated or modified, others will follow suit; and
- secondary activities, which depend on one another and either prepare for a main activity or follow it.

CREATIVITY

Finding solutions to correct or improve procedures is a matter of finding ideas, and that involves creativity.

Asking who, what, where, when, how, and why after each activity starts the generation of ideas. Other techniques produce ideas in great numbers. Two of these are synectics and brainstorming. Briefly, *synectics* is based on free association: creating metaphors and analogies during informal interchanges between individuals in small, selected groups. *Brainstorming* involves the spontaneous contribution of ideas from all members of a group.

LOOKING FOR THE BEST SOLUTION

The third step leads to a number of solutions that can be presented in graphic form. From among these solutions, eventually, one must be chosen. This is the fourth step.

To find the optimal solution to a problem, the problem must be defined and analyzed. Possible solutions must then be examined and a decision made from them.

PROBLEM DEFINITION

A *problem* is a discrepancy between what should be and what is. The discrepancy is always caused by a change of some kind. As long as the nature of that change has not been identified, all efforts to correct the discrepancy will be futile. However, as soon as it has been identified, a solution becomes possible, if not obvious.

Defining a problem, then, involves finding the answers to the following questions:

- What is it? In other words, what is the observed discrepancy? What person, what process, or what object does it affect?
- Where is the problem? Where, exactly, does the discrepancy occur? Where is the system or procedure that causes a problem?
- When does it occur? When, exactly, does the discrepancy occur? When is the system or procedure checked before the problem occurs?
- How many? That is, what is the scope of the problem? How many systems or procedures are affected by this problem?

To define what the problem is not, the same questions may be applied in the negative. For example, ask: what systems are affected and which are not? How many systems or procedures are affected by this problem and how many are not?

The clearer the dividing line between what is and what is not, the better the chances of making the distinctions needed to find the possible causes of the problem.

PRIORITIES

Once the problems to be corrected have been identified, one must choose which to undertake first. Such priorities will depend on the urgency, seriousness, and trend of the problem. To determine the urgency, answer the following questions:

- Is time a critical factor?
- How much time do we have to make a decision?
- Can we use a temporary solution to give us time for a full analysis?
- What will this cost?

The seriousness of the problem may be defined by using the answers to these questions:

- What are the repercussions?

Problem Analysis Sheet				
Discrepancy				
Definition				
	Is	Is not	Distinction	Change
WHAT?				
WHERE is the problem?				
WHEN does it occur?				
HOW MANY? (What is its scope?)				
Possible causes				

FIGURE 5.20 - A PROBLEM ANALYSIS RECORD/SHEET

- What will be the medium- and long-term effects if the problem is not resolved?
- What influence does it have on other persons, resources, departments, safety, and security?
- Will it create other problems?
- What would be the consequences if it is not given high priority?

The following questions may be used to discern the trend of the problem and its direction:

- Is the problem worsening, diminishing, or disappearing?
- What will happen in the future?
- Will the problem grow worse?
- Will it disappear by itself?

Established priorities are not necessarily permanent and final. Their purpose is to set up an initial plan for resolving the problems identified.

PROBLEM ANALYSIS

After the problem has been defined and the distinction between what it is and what it is not has been made, the data may be analyzed to identify clues to its causes.

This analysis process is done in two steps. First, look for the characteristics that distinguish what the problem is from what it is not. What is relevant to what the problem is and what lacks relevance to what it is not? Also, look for a characteristic unique to the part of the system where the problem exists.

Then, look for changes in the zones of distinction. What has changed in the unique distinction or characteristic of that portion of the system where the problem occurs?

An analyst may find a problem analysis record helpful in this process. An example is shown in figure 5.20.

The following story illustrates how easy it is to improve certain things without ever getting to the root of the real problem. It also demonstrates why it is so important to define the problem and analyze it thoroughly.

In a human resources department, an administrative assistant spends a great deal of time recruiting. Sending application forms to possible employees takes so much time that the forms are returning too late for the applicants to be considered.

One BPI/WS analyst looked at the situation and noted that since the personnel turnover had increased considerably, it took nearly half a day per week to buy stamps (to mail the forms) and keep an accounting record of the expenditure. The analyst simplified the accounting system and shortened that time to a few hours per week only. This worked for a while.

A second BPI/WS analyst investigated further. He recommended the purchase of a stamp machine and almost completely eliminated the need for stamps altogether. This saved another two to three hours per week, even though a few stamps were still needed for specific return envelopes.

A few months later, a third BPI/WS analyst recommended the use of postage-paid return envelopes, thereby eliminating stamps altogether. The department declared the recommended improvement a success.

Actually, it was not. A fourth BPI/WS analyst revealed the real problem: personnel turnover that was much too high. She recommended examination and improvement of recruitment and hiring techniques, as well as human resources management policies.

FLOW CHART

A flow chart usually provides the optimal solution. The flow chart clarifies activities and, as a result, allows an analyst to see which can be eliminated and which can be improved. The following exercise is an example.

◆   Exercise

Create a flow chart from this information about a change to an employee's file:

The divisional director's secretary types form 52 in triplicate and puts it on the director's desk. The director examines the document, approves, signs all three for approval, and then returns them to the secretary.

The secretary files part 3 of form 52 alphabetically. The original and copy 2 are sent to the personnel department through internal mail. The personnel department clerk takes the two documents from the in-basket and enters the employee's name and the reason for the change in a register. The clerk telephones the personnel control department to ask for an authorization number to enter on both copies of form 52. The clerk brings both copies to the salary section and puts them in the in-basket. The salary clerk examines the documents, initials them in the appropriate space, and takes them back to the personnel department. The personnel department clerk removes the employee's file from a

PROBLEM ANALYSIS

The seven steps of problem analysis include a series of comparisons of the various parts of the information available, so as to arrive at a most-likely cause-and-effect situation.

<u>Steps 1 and 2</u>

Compare what should be	Work norm	Objectives
with what <u>is</u>	Real output Discrepancy = problem(s)	Order of priority

<u>Steps 3, 4, and 5</u>

Compare what <u>is</u>	Define the problem (what, where, when, how many)	Determine distinctions and changes
with what <u>is not</u>	Describe what is outside the problem (what, where, when, how many)	

<u>Steps 6 and 7</u>

Compare possible causes	Determine the most <u>probable</u> cause

FIGURE 5.21 - SEVEN STEPS OF PROBLEM ANALYSIS

filing cabinet, adds the approved changes, and returns the folder back to the cabinet. The clerk types out form 50, a seven-part "notice of change." He or she compares the new document with form 52 and makes corrections. Next, copies 3, 4, 5, and 6 are distributed, and copy 7 is destroyed. Copies 1 and 2 are sent to the divisional secretary, and both copies of form 52 are destroyed. The divisional secretary compares both copies of form 50 with the copy of form 52 on file before destroying the last copy for form 52.

AN ALTERNATE TO THE FOURTH STEP

An alternate approach to the fourth step foregoes the flow chart in favor of problem identification and analysis. Seven steps are involved in this process (figure 5.21):

Compare the work norm with the real output. A discrepancy between the work norm and the real output constitutes a problem.

Establish an order of priority in the problems according to their urgency; their seriousness; their tendency, trend, direction; and their possibility of getting worse.

Define the problem with the following questions: What is it? Where is it? When does it appear? How big a problem is it?

Determine what the problem is not.

Distinguish what is from what is not.

Deduce the possible causes of the discrepancy observed from the distinguishing factors and the changes noted.

Look for the most probable cause of the discrepancy. Focus on that which can explain all aspects of the problem.

The seven steps of problem analysis include a series of comparisons. Various parts of the information available are weighed against each other, so that a most-likely cause-and-effect situation may be identified.

◆   Case Study

The following is a case study of the reorganization of a secretarial service.

After reorganizing its secretarial service, a large service company was faced with a problem. The secretaries were first ill-at-ease, then dissatisfied, and finally furious. They complained that nothing was working: the word processing machines were worthless, their desks were not at the correct height, the air conditioning was noisy, and management was making wrong decisions. Management tried to clarify the nature of the complaints. This action caused passions to flare, and, as is often the case in such situations, produced little dependable data.

On the other hand, the people affected were easily and precisely identified. It was about one-fifth of the secretarial staff.

By asking where exactly the problem was occurring, it was established that the complaints were coming from the secretaries in the "old" building, and not from all of them. What distinguished the dissatisfied secretaries from the others was the fact that they had been transferred to an old building after the reorganization. Their situation had changed; they now had smaller offices than previously. This change constituted the cause of the problem; the secretaries could not accept the loss of prestige their move represented.

The word processing equipment, the height of the desks, the air conditioning, and management's decisions had little to do with the secretaries' discontent. As long as only the complaints were examined, the analysis of the problem to find its cause did not get very far.

When a distinction was made between what was (the secretaries that complained) from what was not (the secretaries that did not complain) it became possible to resolve the situation.

With a problem analysis sheet, you can do a systematic analysis of the above situation.

How to Choose the Best Solution

An optimum solution can come from a flow chart or from the seven-step technique just described. If there is still doubt, or if there are many possible solutions, there is another technique for evaluating the solutions generated so that the best one will be chosen.

First, make a list of possible solutions. Then, prepare a list of criteria and define them clearly. A *criterion* is a principle used to distinguish the real from the false, to judge, to classify, and so on. To avoid meaningless discussions, each criterion must have the same meaning for all parties concerned.

There are two types of criteria: quantitative and qualitative. *Quantitative criteria* are those based on measurable values such as dimension, weight, quantity produced, speed, and cost. They result in objective decisions.

Qualitative criteria are based on values difficult to measure, such as ease of operation and maintenance, durability, safety, and security. Any decision made based on these criteria most likely will be subjective.

It would be difficult to establish a list of all the criteria necessary for evaluating possible solutions. Criteria vary according to the kind of problem, the urgency of the situation, or the type of company. It is nevertheless possible to group them according to their subject. A few examples are discussed below.

◆   Economic Criteria

These affect everything that deals with the cost a solution may entail. They include:
- acquisition cost;
- administration cost;
- insurance cost;
- maintenance cost; and
- exploitation cost.

Generally, economic factors have top priority because of their importance in the survival of a company. However, there are situations when other criteria come first. In the aviation field, for example, safety comes first. The necessity of dealing with an urgent situation can also relegate economic factors to second place. A department that urgently needs to deliver a very heavy piece of equipment, might not hesitate to ask for its delivery by air.

The *total cost concept* must also be taken into account. This means all the costs the solution would entail. Procedure or system changes made in one area of the company often have an impact or repercussions in other parts of the company. An improvement in one department may occur at the expense of another department. It is even possible that an improvement in one department may cause an overall increase in the corporate expenses.

◆   Technical Criteria

These concern everything involving equipment, including service, its products, and the material it uses.

◆   Human Criteria

These are internal factors, such as safety, working conditions, workforce qualifications, attitude of the union, and how personnel react. They are also external factors such as the role and the responsibility of the company towards the community, including the environment.

LIST THE CRITERIA

The third step is to list the criteria in order of importance. All criteria

Criteria	Weight	Gross AND Balanced Scores					Comments
		A	B	C	D	E	
1							
2							
3							
4							
5							
Etc.							
Total							

FIGURE 5.22 - EVALUATION TABLE

do not have the same value. For example, in choosing a machine, its appearance should not have the same importance as its ease and speed of operation. One must therefore establish an order of importance.

All the criteria listed will more or less affect the chosen plan of action. Some will be vital; others will have a considerable effect, some just so-so, and a few will not affect the outcome very much. The first ones should be considered *criteria of necessity*, the second, *criteria of usefulness*, and the third present a *certain interest*. After discarding the criteria that are simply interesting, a distinction between what is necessary and what is useful must be made. This distinction helps avoid an option that may have little effect later on. What is necessary, we cannot do without; what is useful would be desirable to have or to get. The concept of usefulness clarifies the advantages and the inconveniences in relative terms.

The necessary criteria must be kept. As for the useful ones, one must weigh them. Assign each one a certain number of points according to their relative importance, based on experience. The most important criterion gets ten points; the rest receive points relative to the first (9-8-7-6-etc. or 8-6-4-2).

The criteria retained may then be listed in order of importance.

The fourth step is to evaluate each possible solution in accordance with each criterion. They may be numbered or balanced on the list, or an evaluation chart like that in figure 5.22 may be used.

To use the evaluation chart:
- enter the criteria and their weight (balance points);
- identify each solution with a letter;
- evaluate each solution in relation with each criterion, the solution that best meets the criterion gets 10 and the others get less relative to the first one, and indicate the gross score obtained in the upper corner of the space;
- multiply the gross score by the weight and show the balanced score in the bottom corner; and
- add each solution's balanced scores.

The optimum solution will be the one with the highest score. The analyst may then proceed to the next work simplification step.

IMPLEMENTATION

The fifth step is the planning, completion, and control of the activities involved in implementing the chosen solution. This is true whether it is an improvement or a change in the procedure or system.

To plan activities well, it is necessary to:
- make up the list of the activities needed to bring about the improvement or change;
- determine the sequence of these activities, and the order in which they must be performed;
- set the duration of these activities; and
- prepare the execution timetable or program, i.e., fix the dates and the deadlines for the activities, taking into account the necessary and available resources.

Carrying out the activities means respecting the execution timetable. It is imperative to control, i.e., check if the planned activities have been done in accordance with the program.

An analyst should not overestimate the benefits of the new system or procedure proposed. It is best to stick to the moderate assertions that can be proven. Applying too much pressure can have adverse results. It is preferable to persuade management to implement the new system or procedure in steps rather than pressing for the whole project to be accepted at once and risk being refused.

An analyst must also recognize the weaknesses of the new system, if there are any, and be ready to admit to them when presenting it and during subsequent meetings. It is wise to forewarn management that production will probably decrease at the beginning of the new system's implementation. A trial period usually is necessary. Time is also needed for people to alter work habits and let the new system show what it can do.

Planning the implementation may be done on a Gantt chart or by using the critical path method or PERT chart.

After implementation, it is time to examine the new system or procedure. That is the final step of work simplification.

FOLLOW-UP

In the sixth step of work simplification, the new system or procedure is evaluated by comparing the actual results with those expected. This is done to:
- apply necessary corrective measures, if needed;
- anticipate difficulties; and
- draw the maximum advantage from the changes made.

First, define the objectives and the evaluation standards or points of comparison, to determine:
- what is to be controlled;
- the unit of measure and the limits of the control;

- the frequency of the follow-ups; and
- the control points.

It is important to measure real results. Continuous evaluation or the use of survey methods allows exact data for each chosen standard to be obtained. Comparing real results to the standards determines if there are important differences between the actual results and those anticipated. When there is a considerable gap between what is and what was expected, there is a need for a thorough analysis.

What remains, then, is a decision about which corrective measures should be taken and how to apply them. It may be a question of correcting the system, the procedure, or even the standards, if they were not properly established or if the system or procedure cannot be modified.

At this stage, analysts come full circle, in the sense that a marked gap between real and anticipated results can lead to a completely or partially new study of the system or procedure.

CONCLUSION

In every step of work simplification, the keys to success are the questions that are asked and answered. These lead to important solutions. Many of these questions have been outlined and discussed in this chapter. However, there are always more. Some additional questions to ask when examining the graphical by-products of the six steps are listed below.

When reviewing a system flow chart, these are some of the questions that should be answered:

- Are all the process steps in the system necessary?
- Are all the activities of the system necessary for it to function well?
- Are the overall system objectives and that of each procedure realistic?
- Do they correspond to those of the company?
- Is the material necessary for the good functioning of the system available or must we buy it?
- Do we have enough information and resources?
- Is everything we have necessary?

A process flow chart should generate the answers to these questions:

- Is the process step or function really necessary?
- Is each main activity of the procedure necessary? Does it occur at the proper time?

- Are the presentation, the order, and the quality of the information satisfactory?
- Is each form necessary? Is it prepared at the right time? Does the manner of completion suit the person using it, and the use made of it? Is each part or copy of the form necessary?
- Is each file (file folder, register, journal, etc.) necessary? Is each kept in the right place? Is it kept by the person who needs it?
- Is each operation necessary and done at the best time in the process? Could we combine it with other similar operations? Is it done by the most qualified person?
- Is each control necessary and done at the best stage of the process? Could we combine it with other similar controls? Is it done by the most qualified person?
- Would it be possible to reduce the number of moves between desks by modifying the layout? Is all the traveling necessary and justified?
- Could we eliminate or reduce waiting time?
- When the volume warrants it, could we use machines? Could we regroup work to justify mechanization or automation?

While reviewing a flow diagram, consider these questions:

- Is the flow in a straight line that avoids detours, backtracking, and cross checking?
- Have we studied the flow of other systems and procedures?
- Have we reduced the space allocated to private offices to a minimum?
- Was the space allocated using criteria other than the hierarchy?
- Have we taken into account person-to-person and person-to-equipment relationships in space arrangements?
- Have we taken into account the light reflection phenomena in the choice of material and colors?
- Have we reduced the noise level as much as possible?
- Have the desks been placed so they do not face windows, entrances, aisles, and other desks? Are they in line with air conditioning ducts?
- Are the aisles sufficiently wide to allow for normal traffic?
- In the arrangement of private offices, have the nature of the

work, its confidentiality, and the security of documents been
taken into account?
- Have fire protection regulations been considered?
- Has the layout been evaluated according to space utilization
  factors?
- Have the proposed changes been the object of a cost/benefit
  analysis?

Some of these questions apply to specific components of work
processes and systems that are not necessarily easily addressed during
the six work simplification steps. The following chapters will examine
these in more detail. What is important to remember is that a questioning,
curious attitude is key in developing a reliable, optimum process or
system.

6

FORMS

A form is a document on which permanent data is printed. It also includes blank space for the entry of other data. The form registers facts and transmits information, permitting the exercise of control. The information it generates is relayed to those working on the task at hand and the supervisors of the tasks being done or completed. There are three types of forms:

- the simple form, a single page or several sheets without carbon paper;
- the roll form, a certain number of sheets with carbon paper glued to them at one end; and
- the continuous form, a certain number of sheets, with carbon paper, usually used for computer printing and word processing.

Why are there so many forms in offices today? Forms are used to make up for the lack of knowledge and competence. In forms, untrained employees find the rules and information they need to do their work. Filling out a form reassures them. The greater their ignorance, the more forms they use. Fear of change also generates piles of forms. These piles in turn constitute a rigid framework behind which employees can hide. This rigid framework limits the creation of an influence network.

Changes in the workforce distribution since 1800 have also contributed to the proliferation of forms. In 1800, ninety-five percent of the workforce was agricultural; in 1985, this number was 3 percent. Today, the number of office workers greatly surpasses farm workers and factory workers combined. The ratio of office employees to factory workers in the western world has gone from 1 to 5 (1935), to 1 to 4 (1950), to 1 to 1 (1965), to 2 to 1 (1985).

The redistribution of the workforce has come from an increase in office work, which leads to an escalating use of forms. Of course, offices should use forms. The function of office work, after all, is to collect, use, file, review, and disseminate internal and external data. However, the number of forms that various functions produce should be limited, so that workers are not asphyxiated under a mountain of paperwork. How can this be done?

Before creating a form, it is essential to ask the following questions:
- Why create a new form if one exists for the same purpose?
- Why not use an existing one that plays the same role?
- Will the use of the new form make the work more accurate or more economical?
- Could the contemplated form be integrated into an existing form?
- Could the contemplated form eliminate other forms?
- Has the contemplated form been presented to its future users to get their comments?

DESIGNING A FORM

To create a form, it is imperative to know what it will be used for and how to make it fulfill that role. Thus, it must be determined:
- who will use it;
- where it will be used;
- how it will be filled out (in writing, by hand, with a typewriter or a word processor, or a computer); and
- why (to what end or for what purpose it is being created).

Other elements also must be taken into consideration. Some examples are eliminating all unnecessary details, combining forms *in toto* or in part, regrouping the purchase of related forms, and standardizing the formats.

One must also consider the typography and character of the form, critically analyzing it with a focus on three factors: efficiency, appearance, and cost. To decide whether the form is efficient or not, apply work simplification and work study techniques.

For appearance, decide whether the form is easy to identify. A form's appearance can only be analyzed when it has been filled out. A blank form is of little use; only when a form is complete does it start fulfilling its purpose. A well-balanced utilization of data, color, number of copies, lines, blank, and shaded spaces will all contribute to appearance.

For cost analysis, forms must be evaluated. A simple model (fig. 6.1) illustrates the three cost elements of all entry management systems. To reach the cost reduction objective, and thereby raise profits, systems analysis and work simplification techniques should be applied to the three elements shown in figure 6.1. These three elements are:

- the process surrounding the use of forms: the entry work, handling, distribution, filing, and others. It is the element with the greatest possibilities of cost reduction or savings;
- the entry mode, which can be anything from a pencil to a sophisticated computer with a high speed printer; and
- the forms: any piece of paper on which one enters (by hand or machine) data or information that will be read by other persons or machines.

There is a widespread belief that computerization of paperwork in itself leads to appreciable savings. Anyone who has noted the mounds of computer-produced printouts that are never again reviewed quite rightly questions this naive belief about savings and the so-called "paperless" office.

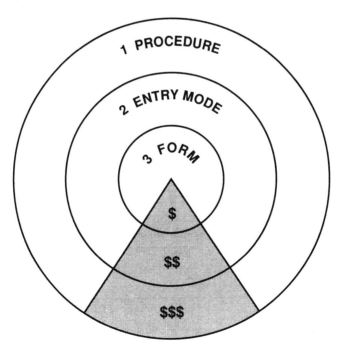

FIGURE 6.1 - A SIMPLE MODEL OF THE THREE COST ELEMENTS OF ALL ENTRY MANAGEMENT SYSTEMS

Actually, it does not matter whether one feeds preprinted forms into a computer printer, has the computer produce the forms, or refers to the data on video screens. An experienced analyst does not focus on forms, but instead examines the process and entry modes. Only after exhausting these areas should attention be turned to forms, whether or not they are computerized.

The most important quality of a form is being easy-to-read. When designing the form, follow these steps:

- use simple language with a minimum of words;
- put the titles above the data;
- use lines or shaded spaces as reading guides;
- use shaded spaces to increase or diminish the importance of the data;
- highlight sections with color codes;
- number the entries so they are easy to find;
- group related data;
- group data that needs special attention; and
- use both colored ink and colored paper.

Paper is an important factor. Printers use standard format, ready-cut rolls of paper. Photocopiers use the same formats. It is preferable, therefore, to standardize the size of the form. Thought should also be given to the thickness and quality of the paper. How often will it be handled? Does it have a conservation deadline? Should it be acid-free? There are also special papers that meet specific needs: business cards, labels, identity cards, checks, and so on. A printer can help make that choice.

The color of the paper is important. The judicious use of different colors will make dispatching, filing, and distributing copies easier. The color becomes a code: recognizing a color takes less time than reading a title.

The contrast between what carbon paper leaves on a copy and the color of the paper determines how readable a form is. The lightest color should be the last copy of a multipart form, since the carbon imprint is less visible at that point.

There are different kinds of carbon paper. Some is hard and glazed, for two or three copies. Certain papers are only partly carbonized to allow only the information that is needed in that particular copy to be imprinted.

Self-copying, or no carbon required (NCR), paper is ordinary paper that has been chemically treated to reproduce onto a.subsequent copy.

It is used mostly where the use of carbon paper would be inconvenient. It is also available in different colors and is fully or partially treated. The use of NCR paper has its disadvantages. For example, because of its rough surface, two or three sheets may attach themselves to each other and create serious filing problems. Its thickness limits the number of copies per document. The chemical treatment tends, over time, to disappear.

The choice of ink colors is up to the form designer and may vary considerably. Print shops, however, use black and gray as basic colors and will impose a surcharge for any other colors.

To make a form easy-to-complete:
- eliminate all that is unnecessary;
- preprint the instructions;
- use boxes that may be checked off;
- use abbreviations and codes;
- plan for continuous writing;
- adopt a left-to-right and top-to-bottom order;
- make a provision for a normal left margin;
- group the answers to be filled in;
- use lines or shaded spaces as writing guides;
- put items in order, with the data most frequently provided toward the top of the page;
- follow the same order as the source document;
- reduce unnecessary spaces; and
- use window, ordinary, or personalized envelopes.

To make a form easy to manipulate:
- identify pages with titles, numbers, and so on;
- vary the sizes of different parts;
- take into account the order of the different parts;
- use consecutive numbering;
- use complete or partial perforation;
- put a tear-off part either at the bottom or on the side or use a double tear-off part;
- use self-adhesive paper; and
- use forms-handling material.

To assemble copies of the same form, glue them together, staple them together, or glue some and staple others. Some may also be left free in a pile. Punching holes in the forms so that they may be placed in two- or three-ring or spoke binders should be done at the printing stage to lower costs.

Whether a perforated dotted line offers more or less resistance depends on its purpose. Is it there to detach part of the form or assist in folding it? Perforated lines that separate part of the form are placed on a horizontal axis for removing a horizontal part of the form or vertically for a vertical removal. They may also be partially horizontal and vertical (for tearing off a label) or at an angle (for tearing off at a staple so that taking carbons does not disturb the order of the copies).

A forms designer must also wrest maximum advantage from the use of mechanical, electronic, automatic or semiautomatic office machines; typewriters; word processors; computers; and filing methods.

To take advantage of the typewriters and word processors, use:
- normal or special spacing;
- automatic spacing or line search;
- tabs and backspacing; and
- repetitive printing and programming.

RETENTION

From its very creation, a document's retention deadline must be established. Most countries have laws that detail how long, after their use, certain documents must be kept. In Canada, such laws exist on both federal and provincial levels, and they may differ from one another. Similar laws exist in most of the states in the U.S.

It may not be necessary to keep a document in its original form. After a while, it may be permissible to record it on microfiche, microfilm, or compact disk. The conversion costs are very often minimal compared to the costs of archiving paper. One must keep a note on a retention calendar for paper, electronic, or other documents.

Specialists in records management keep track of such timetables, and BPI/WS analysts may participate in setting them up.

FORMS ANALYSIS CHART

To eliminate duplicate and unnecessary forms and to revise others, a *forms analysis chart* may be used. This chart groups, on a single sheet, the column headings of those forms being examined.

To complete the chart illustrated in figure 6.2:
- enter, in the column headings, the title and number of the forms to be compared;
- sum up in the "headings" column, the object of each heading for the first form;
- check off each heading in the first column;

Forms analysis chart	Title:																
Form or operation																	
Analysis / Date																	TOTAL
HEADINGS	No	No	No	No	No	No	No	No	No	No	No	No	No	No	No	No	
1																	
2																	
3																	
4																	
5																	
6																	
7																	
8																	
9																	
10																	
11																	
12																	
13																	
14																	
15																	
16																	
17																	
18																	
19																	
20																	
21																	
22																	
23																	
24																	
TOTAL																	

FIGURE 6.2 - FORMS ANALYSIS CHART

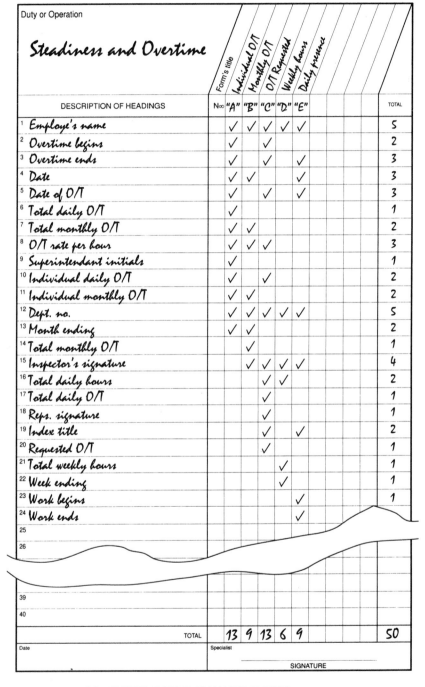

Duty or Operation: Steadiness and Overtime	Individual O/T	Monthly O/T	O/T Requested	Weekly hours	Daily presence					TOTAL
DESCRIPTION OF HEADINGS / N∞	"A"	"B"	"C"	"D"	"E"					TOTAL
1 Employe's name	✓	✓	✓	✓	✓					5
2 Overtime begins	✓		✓							2
3 Overtime ends	✓		✓	✓						3
4 Date	✓	✓		✓						3
5 Date of O/T	✓		✓	✓						3
6 Total daily O/T	✓									1
7 Total monthly O/T	✓	✓								2
8 O/T rate per hour	✓	✓	✓							3
9 Superintendant initials	✓									1
10 Individual daily O/T	✓		✓							2
11 Individual monthly O/T	✓	✓								2
12 Dept. no.	✓	✓	✓	✓	✓					5
13 Month ending	✓	✓								2
14 Total monthly O/T		✓								1
15 Inspector's signature		✓	✓	✓	✓					4
16 Total daily hours			✓	✓						2
17 Total daily O/T		✓								1
18 Reps. signature		✓								1
19 Index title		✓		✓						2
20 Requested O/T		✓								1
21 Total weekly hours				✓						1
22 Week ending				✓						1
23 Work begins					✓					1
24 Work ends					✓					
25										
26										
39										
40										
TOTAL	13	9	13	6	9					50

Date   Specialist

SIGNATURE

FIGURE 6.3 - COMPLETED FORMS ANALYSIS CHART

- in the second column, check off each heading of the second form that is similar to the first form;
- in the headings column, add the headings that are not in the first form. Check off the last ones in the second column; and
- proceed in the same fashion for all forms entered in the chart headings.

Figure 6.3 illustrates a completed forms analysis chart. Preparing such a chart may result in the following:

- the elimination of unnecessary forms;
- the elimination of unnecessary headings;
- combined forms;
- the elimination of unnecessary words and sentences; and
- the standardizing of text.

CONCLUSION

As with any work simplification task, the proper evaluation of forms includes asking a number of penetrating questions. The following should be asked about any forms design, revision, or management system:

- When creating the form, have we taken into account: 1) the relative order of the information on the original document; 2) how the form is completed; 3) sorting, filing, and referencing requirements; 4) the appropriate type of paper, its use and preservation; and 5) the important elements?
- Does the form serve the purpose for which it was created?
- Does it duplicate another?
- If it is to be typed, does the layout suit the typewriter or computer?
- Is it numbered?
- Are there instructions for its use?
- Are the instructions on the form itself?
- Are the instructions still visible when the form is in the typewriter?
- Would it be better to have an additional copy instead of transcribing the information to some other form or register?
- Is each piece of information requested actually useful?
- Could we preprint some important information?
- Is there enough space to enter the information?

COMMUNICATIONS
AND REPORTS

In addition to preparing reports about or for the current study, analysts and consultants must very often evaluate the quality of reports prepared by others. They will also be called upon to explain, orally or in writing, what they are recommending. Therefore, they must be good communicators and report writers.

GENERAL CONSIDERATIONS

One of the greatest problems in society today is the lack of or poor communications. Yet, in all management processes, there is an overriding principle: always communicate the objectives to all team members.

What is communication? *Communication* is letting someone know about something through a common system of symbols. It establishes a relationship with someone. It is also an action and an object.

This common system of symbols is very important; the same language must be spoken. If the language of this book suddenly became French, Spanish, or Italian, many readers would be lost.

One communication theory suggests that if all verbal or written exchanges in a social group were eliminated, that group would cease to exist. The communication of ideas and information maintains the group as such.

In most verbal communications, there are often three messages:
- what was said;
- what the listener thinks was said; and
- what the speaker meant to say.

For example, in a meeting, one person makes a statement and

another replies only to have the first speaker say "No, no, what I meant to say was. . . . "Or, if someone were asked to write "seventy three forty two" in numerals, what would he or she write? 7342, 70 3 42, 73 40 2, or what else?

Not only are there three messages in most conversations but the same words also will not have the same meaning for everybody. Some years ago, a study at Columbia University uncovered that there are 500 English words that have a total of 14,000 meanings. (For example, Webster's dictionary lists 73 meanings for the word "round.")

A communication is successful when both the sender and the receiver reach a meeting of the mind.

THE ELEMENTS OF COMMUNICATION
There are three elements in communication:

SENDER — MESSAGE — RECEIVER

The sender has the most responsibility of the three. He or she must make sure the message is understood. Most senders rely on verbal communication, which may be characterized as one- or two-way.

One-way communication is faster and more orderly than two-way communication. It gives the sender more satisfaction along with a feeling of power. However, one-way communication generally requires more preparation than two-way communication.

Two-way communication is more precise than one-way communication. The receiver, able to react, is more likely to feel confident about understanding. The sender remains alert because the receiver(s) will indicate when the message is not clear.

Establishing good two-way communication is not easy. A sender must be ready to make an effort. Also, two-way communication will become one-way if the sender appears hard to please, sarcastic, or uncooperative. Similarly, one-way communication will result if the receiver refuses to collaborate. In such cases, the sender must make every effort to alter the receiver's attitude.

So, when trying to convince people of something, a sender should present things in a manner that will be acceptable to them. Before they can be ready to accept anything, they are very likely to ask themselves: "What's in it for me [WIIFM]?"

NONVERBAL COMMUNICATION

Nonverbal communication consists of gestures and facial expressions, as well as dress. For example, the "punk" generation has used a dress code to communicate opposition to society.

There are times when verbal and nonverbal communications send contradictory messages. Whether it is intentional or not, ordinary language can communicate not only ideas but feelings and emotions as well. A message often has an obvious content (the accepted meaning of the words) and a hidden content (the meaning that the sender gave to the words in the message). "Is that really what he or she meant?" is a useful question to ask oneself and sometimes the sender.

THE QUALITIES OF GOOD COMMUNICATION

There are specific qualities necessary for good communication to take place. Four of these are:
- commitment;
- a clear statement;
- a varied presentation of ideas; and
- empathy.

Emerson said: "Nothing great has ever been done without enthusiasm." If a speaker does not believe in what he or she is saying or writing, he or she should stop. Enthusiasm is communicative. Jean-Marc Chaput, a noted expert who conducts seminars on motivation asks pointedly: "Do you believe in what you are doing?" In short, good communication is all a question of personal commitment. It generates enthusiasm and encourages clear expression and a varied presentation of ideas.

To express him- or herself clearly, a speaker needs to take the time to think about what he or she will say. If necessary, take notes or draw up a written outline. Think about the explanations necessary to reach a communication objective.

As much as possible, a sender should be on the same level as the person for whom the message is intended. To achieve this, pay attention to what the recipient has to say. In written communication, knowledge of the person being addressed is important, as is anticipation of his or her reactions.

Empathy is the faculty of putting oneself in the other person's shoes. A good communicator makes a listener feel unique. A good communicator cares about co-workers. It is always a big mistake to underestimate anyone.

The qualities necessary for good communications also apply to report writing, for a report is "an instrument of communication, information and management." It represents an "objective and in-depth study of a particular situation or question. It gives the writer the task of assembling the elements and making a judicious analysis, so as to arrive, in most cases, at an opinion, a proposal, and/or at motivated conclusions" (Cajolet-Laganiére, 1983).

A report should grab a reader's attention with a skillful introduction, arouse interest with precise and exact information, explain with critical judgment, convince with pertinent proof, and bring about a decision with concrete proposals.

An author of a report must be impartial when reporting facts and rigorously verify any data presented. The proposals and conclusions offered must be weighed carefully. Efficiency and accuracy are the aim.

A report reflects the breadth of the writer's professional knowledge, the soundness of his or her judgment, the acuity of analysis, the soundness of his or her reasoning, and the quality of his or her expression.

The work of an analyst is 10 percent technical and 90 percent persuasion. The analyst must also convince the receiver of the quality of the work and the merits of the proposals. The job of persuasion starts as soon as the study commences. The analyst would do well to put the interested parties in the know immediately because this is the best way to establish an effective working relationship. The analyst must make them follow every step of the way so that they come to the same conclusions. Thus, they will collaborate and accept the analyst's ideas much better; they will feel that the ideas are their own.

Interested parties means not only the supervisor, manager, or receiver, but also all those affected by the report. The receiver will probably be interested in what the assistants and subordinates think of the proposals. Hence the importance of assuring the goodwill of all.

It is not enough to have effective interviews, gather pertinent data, do a meticulous analysis, or even be able to write up a good report; one must master the presentation of ideas.

The report must contain only well chosen information. Thus, it is important to know as precisely as possible the expectations of those receiving the report regarding scope, content, and the spirit in which it was written. The receiver will want to know:
- what the problem is;
- the scope of the study;

- the solution to the problem; and
- the expected benefits.

To this end, it sometimes is essential to meet with the receiver(s).

The receiver wants a clear, concise, and well-presented report that quickly supplies its purpose and the solutions proposed by the writer. The answers to questions should be easy to find in the table of contents, the index, or the help of titles and subtitles.

Most often, the receiver of a BPI/WS analyst's report is someone in management. There are particular considerations to take when a member of management is receiving a report. A manager is rarely satisfied and consequently demands improvement and effective control. To this end, the manager wants to:

- know what is going on and keep subordinates well informed to guide them;
- be sure that the department works according to modern procedures and at the lowest possible cost;
- be sure that the subordinates work well and know how to make good decisions;
- delegate added responsibilities with confidence;
- have clear and precise written policies; and
- be able to compare the results obtained with those expected.

The objectives of a good report are summarized in figure 7.1.

THE QUALITIES OF A GOOD REPORT

To meet the demands of the receiver, a good report must have the following qualities:

- it should be based on concrete facts, be part of a whole, retain only the essential, and present the facts as clearly and accurately as possible;
- it should be characterized by a rigorously logical approach that stems from a systematic analysis of facts and data and ends with the appropriate comments and interpretations; and
- it should present practical and justified conclusions and recommendations that address the problems identified initially.

Of all the information gathered, use only what is essential but carefully keep the rest in a working file. It may be used later to establish purchasing criteria, to create forms, and help with other tasks.

The next consideration is the method of presentation. What tools will be used? Examples are: samples, models, photos, lay models, charts, diagrams, organization charts, overhead slides, 35mm slides, and films.

An analysis report often includes many abstract notions that need to become as tangible as possible. Clearly expressing them orally is a good start, but writing them clearly is better. However, expressing them graphically will have the most impact and can clarify a study. Audiovisual material is an almost indispensable component, whether or not the oral report is followed by a written one.

An analyst attempting to communicate recommendations faces several interesting challenges today. First, because of the pace of business activity, there is a demand that process improvement recommendations be available yesterday at the latest. Secondly, there is a need for complex analyses and conclusions to be presented in a comprehensible format. Many senior executives do not have the time and inclination to follow analytical logic step-by-step.

Thirdly, video and advertising graphics have set a high standard for visual communications. While no one expects an analyst to produce presentations that match the work of media networks and advertising agencies, there is still an unconscious tendency to use it as a standard. Unless the presentation being made comes reasonably close to what executives see through other media, there is a risk that second-rate graphics will also suggest that the analysis is also less than first rate.

Fortunately, there are now a number of computer software packages

---

REPORT OBJECTIVES

1. ATTRACT ATTENTION	through a skillful introduction
2. AROUSE INTEREST	with precise and exact information
3. EXPLAIN	with critical judgment
4. CONVINCE	with pertinent proofs
5. BRING TO A DECISION	with concrete proposals

FIGURE 7.1 - SUMMARY OF GOOD REPORT OBJECTIVES

that enable a neophyte to produce first-rate results. To produce effective presentations in today's environment, it is imperative that the professional analyst or consultant have absolute mastery over one or more of these packages.

No one software package is recommended over the others. Some are more suited to some tasks than others. A little research should enable the analyst to locate one that meets their organization's particular challenges. Moreover, software evolves so rapidly that any recommendation would be out of date before this book could be printed.

When presenting a new system (or a new procedure), it is useful to articulate proposals in the following fashion:
- facts relative to the "old" system;
- drawbacks of the "old" system;
- facts relative to the "new" system; and
- benefits of the "new "system.

WRITING A REPORT
There are five preparatory steps in report writing:
- establishing the precise scope of the subject;
- preparing a provisional work plan;
- gathering the material;
- analyzing and sorting the material; and
- preparing a detailed plan.

ESTABLISHING THE SCOPE OF THE SUBJECT
The writer must know the precise mandate, the objectives of the report, and the purposes the report will serve.

The type of report must also be determined. Is it an explanatory report that describes and demonstrates objectively a certain number of facts or findings? Or is it a critical report that weighs and judges facts to arrive at a proposal? The writer must be sure of the needs and expectations of the receivers.

PREPARING A PROVISIONAL WORK PLAN
The goal of a work plan unearths the various aspects to consider and the different approaches to use, so that all the important angles of the problem may be separated and studied. Very often, a simple analysis of the subject in itself provides a provisional work plan.

A writer may use the table of contents from work on the subject to draw up a plan. In such a case, the particular aspects of the situation at hand must not be forgotten.

GATHERING THE MATERIAL

To gather material, the writer prepares a list of all the resources available: reports, studies, surveys, tests, analysis results, data banks, and specialists' points of view. Each resource must be evaluated according to the date, scope, and accuracy of the data, the originator's reputation, and so on. Above all, it is important to know whether to look for facts or ideas based on facts.

To find and describe facts, a simple and effective method is to note them on small cards or sheets of paper—one for each distinct component. Each card is given a title that identifies it with a part of the provisional research plan. If prepared with care and attention, these cards or sheets will help with the preparation of the detailed plan and perhaps with the actual writing of the report.

ANALYZING AND SORTING THE MATERIAL

After finding and describing the facts, the writer should analyze and sort them, forming ideas and judgments. Then, the observations, ideas, deductions, and judgments should be described in complete sentences. Facts should be separated from ideas, and the leading ideas should be determined.

PREPARING A DETAILED PLAN

To determine the leading ideas that constitute the backbone of the report, the writer must be guided by the subject and the objectives, as well as the expectations of the receiver. The ideas retained must express, with accuracy, the thoughts of the writer while explaining the subject. When combined, these ideas must constitute an answer to the problems that have been defined in the provisional research plan.

For each leading idea, there are three operations: first, to bring out the facts; second, to analyze, explain, and evaluate them; and third, to provide a partial conclusion.

The writer must progress through the ideas in such a way that, in the end, the reader will readily accept the proposals and recommendations. Various types of progress paths are:
- *chronological progression* (a succession of events in time);
- *progression by opposition* (thesis, antithesis, synthesis);
- *progression by theme* (regrouping of elements by category); and

- *quantitative progression* (growing order, decreasing order, from the general to the particular, etc.).

Particular attention must be paid to transitions. These should take the reader effortlessly from one idea to another and naturally lead to an acceptable conclusion.

A precise and well-structured plan builds solid arguments and produces a conclusive report. It demands time and effort, but if done properly, it will cut the writing part of the job in half.

STRUCTURING THE OVERALL REPORT

A letter of introduction should be used to reiterate the object and to remind the receiver of the objectives and the importance of the questions studied. It may also cite a few important aspects of the proposals. A short note at the top of the report could replace the letter of introduction.

Except for the letter of introduction, a report is usually made up of five parts:
- the preliminaries;
- the introduction;
- the development;
- the conclusion; and
- the back matter.

Depending upon the nature and complexity of the report, the preliminary pages, numbered in lower case roman numerals (or not at all), include:
- title page;
- acknowledgment page;
- summary;
- table of contents;
- list of charts;
- list of illustrations; and
- list of abbreviations and acronyms.

The title of the report is extremely important. The title page must have information that will allow the reader to understand the objective of the report, its origin, and its benefits. One way to choose a good title is to list the benefits that the report proposes and select the most important one in the eyes of the reader. Then, express that benefit with three or four striking words.

The introduction must lead the reader to the development portion without revealing it or the conclusion. (If the report is short, the introduction may be replaced with a short note entitled "Subject.") It presents the report's objective, gives it a frame of reference, and raises the reader's interest. It should also support the report's structure based on the table of contents. It is strongly recommended that the final version of the introduction be written only after the report has been completed. That way, it is much easier to highlight the report's key elements.

The development (fig. 7.2) is divided in chapters that should be grouped in two or more parts. These parts should have titles that agree with the subject(s) being discussed. Each chapter has its own introduction, development, and conclusion.

If the detailed plan has been prepared correctly, the writer need only follow it according to the chosen mode of progression. The first main idea starts the development, which then presents the facts arranged according to secondary ideas. Next, the facts are analyzed (justifications, explanations, findings, judgments) and a partial conclusion is drawn.

Through a good transition, the second main idea is introduced. It is developed in the same manner as the first, and the remainder of the development continues accordingly.

To clarify and convince, the writer should use charts, diagrams, drawings, and other illustrations in the text, or if they occupy a great deal of space, in the appendices.

Numbering the various ideas is useful. There are several numbering systems. One uses both letters and numbers (1, A, a, and so forth). It is preferable to use a system that employs numbers (fig. 7.3) only (1; 1.1, 1.2; 1.1.1, 1.1.2, etc.) because it is simpler. Mixing both letters and numbers can bring confusion. Should not a BPI/WS systems analyst be systematic?

The conclusion is a summary of the report's main points and of the suggestions made throughout. It must inspire action. Therefore, it is important to present the suggestions clearly and according to their importance and urgency.

It is best to propose one solution only and keep the others in reserve in the work papers, together with the reasons they were not offered. The analyst can then respond to anyone who questions why one solution was presented rather than another. Offering too many options can perplex the reader. Should the first recommendation be turned down, it will always be possible to present another one.

It is sometimes necessary to add comments that will clarify the scope of the conclusion, showing it as part of a whole and linking it to other aspects of the problem.

The back matter of the report usually includes addenda and/or appendices, a bibliography, and an index. When documents essential to the understanding of a report go beyond a certain length, it is recommended that they be mentioned briefly in the text and put at the end of the report as addenda or appendices. All documents added at the end of the report must also be listed in the table of contents or in the lists of charts, diagrams, and other illustrations.

There are two types of bibliography. The writer may note only the works he or she consulted in connection with the report, or he or she may produce a comprehensive list of any works that refer to the report's subject matter. In either case, it is permissible to add annotations— personal notes commenting on the content and the value of the works

---

REPORT DEVELOPMENT

First main idea   Facts statement
                                Analysis, explanation, and
                                evaluation of facts
                                Partial conclusion

                        - Transition -

Second main idea   Facts statement
                                Analysis, explanation, and
                                evaluation of facts
                                Partial conclusion

                        - Transition -

Third main idea   Facts statement
                                Analysis, explanation, and
                                evaluation of facts
                                Partial conclusion

                        - Transition -

Etc.

FIGURE 7.2 - STEP-BY-STEP PROCESS OF REPORT DEVELOPMENT

NUMBERING EXAMPLE

1. Main idea

    1.1   Statement of facts

    1.2   Analysis of facts

        1.2.1   Explanation

        1.2.2   Evaluation

    1.3   Partial conclusion

2. Main idea

    2.1   Statement of facts

    2.2   Analysis of facts

        2.2.1   Explanation

        2.2.2   Evaluation

    2.3   Partial conclusion

3. Main idea

    3.1   Statement of facts

    3.2   Analysis of facts

        3.2.1   Explanation

        3.2.2   Evaluation

3.3 Partial conclusion

FIGURE 7.3 - NUMERICAL APPROACH TO REPORT WRITING

in question. It may be useful to arrange the bibliography according to subject matter.

The index is prepared after the report is finished. It is an analytical table of the subjects discussed, persons named, and locations noted in the report. It gives the page where each is mentioned. An index is not always necessary.

COMPOSITION

Writing well is not an ability that can be learned in one day. One only acquires the skill with practice and patience; each attempt improves style on a day-to-day basis. The following ideas should help a writer express him- or herself clearly and accurately in writing. Not only may they be used for reports, but also for internal memos, letters, meeting minutes, and other written pieces.

Before starting, a writer should ask these questions:

- To whom am I writing? (Who is the receiver?)
- For what reaction am I looking? (What is my objective?)
- How will I express my ideas? (What is the content/ structure?)

TO WHOM AM I WRITING?

The writer that wants a message to be understood must think in terms of those receiving the message and adapt the text to them. What do they want to know? What are their personalities, preoccupations? Are they very busy? How much time do they have? Should the message be short or long? Should it include many or few details? Are there special expectations? Do the receivers make the decisions or defer to someone else?

Use language that the receiver(s) can understand. Simple words and short sentences are always preferable to erudite, obscure words, and sentences that do not seem to end.

The style should be lively. Keep any questions short and to the point. Do not use labored expressions, such as "I would be grateful if you could tell me the delivery deadlines providing you have that information." A better expression of that request would be: "What is the delivery deadline?"

FOR WHAT REACTION AM I LOOKING?

What is the purpose of the communication? What is expected from its receivers? What will they do after they receive it? Is that the desired reaction? Make a list of the facts and reasons why the reader should act accordingly. Be clear in the steps that need to be followed.

If the objective of the report is strictly to inform, what information should it give? If the reader is to be convinced of something, the writer must be convinced of the idea's merit.

HOW WILL I EXPRESS MY IDEAS?

Before he or she begins writing, a writer should put on paper the ideas he or she wants to express, making a list of the subjects to present. The main idea or theme to be communicated should be presented clearly and with emphasis. This will help a writer arrange text in a logical order.

As long as the text remains clear and simple, a writer should not be afraid to express personality. A personal or humorous remark helps break the monotony of a dry text and maintains the reader's attention. Too many plays on words or heavy jokes should be avoided, however.

Adapt the length of the sentences to the message being communicated. Short and direct sentences convey simple ideas. Readers will more easily grasp an idea if the writer's style goes directly to the crux of the matter. Reread sentences of more than twenty-five words; there is surely a way to shorten them.

On the other hand, longer sentences may be necessary in establishing a connection between more than one idea. Use *thus, and, so that, for,* and *because* to indicate the links between different ideas.

Use the active, direct voice where possible. "We hired M. X. on January 20," is generally a better format than "M. X. was hired on the 20th of January." Also, "the study demonstrates that" is preferable to "after an in-depth study of the situation, it is evident that . . ." (which is also grammatically incorrect).

A writer should always reread his or her first draft to eliminate useless words and expressions. Remove redundancies (such as "mutual collaboration"), pompous expressions (e.g., "notwithstanding the fact that" vs. "as") and superfluous repetition of ideas.

There is no room for jargon in a well-written report or document. Demonstrating a great knowledge of professional terminology is unnecessary. Technical jargon only makes the text harder to read: it does not make it lighter or easier.

Limit superlatives. It is difficult to believe a text full of "magificents," "excellents," and "superbs," unless good reasons justify the use of them. "Very" is another overused word that should be avoided. It distracts from the meaning of the word it modifies.

Avoid maxims, which rarely belong in an administrative text. However, they may be used as chapter headings when appropriate, which is rare.

Limit relative pronouns. They make it more difficult to read and understand a sentence. It is often better to write two sentences than to use several pronouns.

Avoid long strings of prepositional phrases. Too many "ofs," "ins," and "throughs," are confusing. For example: "Treat each location one after the other in the order that seems best for communicating your message." "Treat each location in sequence" would be better.

After deciding the content and the ideas that are to be communicated, a writer can organize his or her writing several ways. One method is to use logical sequence to describe an administrative procedure such as the flow of a payment request or a series of operations for how a gadget is made. Successive steps of a procedure determine divisions of the text.

Another method is organizing by geographical location, or by describing what happens in different places. For example: discuss what must be done or what needs to be done in the offices, then a region, then a state. Treat each location one after another.

A desirable organizational strategy for reports that propose changes is by recommendation and the reasons for it. Lay out arguments in the following order:

- what is essential;
- why (facts and reasons);
- how; and
- when (set out the deadline).

If the ideas developed do not allow organization by one of the above methods, take each idea separately. Establish an order of priority, then decide whether to start with the most important and continue in decreasing order of importance or vice-versa. Often, the main idea dictates the order to follow, all others being subordinate to it. In such cases, the plan will organize itself. However, do not forget the reader's logic; it may be different.

Only put one idea in a paragraph. Each time the subject or idea changes, start a new one. The last paragraph should be used to indicate what action the reader should take next. The report should not end without specifying what should happen next.

◆ Exercise

The above information may be applied to the following exercise.

Rewrite the following text, eliminating partial nuances and ideas that are too general. Replace them with objective remarks and simple and well-considered expressions. Correct spelling errors and punctuation.
Time allowed: 15 minutes

> *The study clearly brought out the office's inefficiency, that the procedures in use created waste of time and duplication and that reports and files contained errors. That entries were never checked, that the terminals were only used about one quarter of their capacity, that the employees spent part of their time reading newspapers, that they showed little interest for their work. Despite their good will they are fed up and no one seems to know why he/she works and what purpose does their work have. In short the situation leaves a lot to be desired and it is surprising that the losses for the year are only $12,000 as shown in the accounting books.*

The above text could have been written as follows:

> *Here is what our study revealed:*
> * *the work methods resulted in loss of time and duplication;*
> * *reports and files had numerous errors;*
> * *no one checked entries; and*
> * *terminals operated at only 25 percent capacity.*
> *Employees showed little interest in their work because they do not know its purpose. In such a situation, it is surprising that business losses were only $12,000.*

PHYSICAL PRESENTATION

Preparing a report takes time and effort. Why spoil its quality with a poor presentation? Particular attention should therefore be given to the following items:
* protecting the document with a good binding or a title page in the case of a short report;
* if it is a large report, putting fly-leaves at the beginning and end;
* producing a table of contents for all reports more than two pages long;
* choosing a clear and simple type style; and

- making sure that charts, diagrams, and illustrations are well prepared and have appropriate titles.

An analysis report generally interests more than one person. Therefore, make sure that there is a sufficient number of copies for distribution.

The success of a study depends largely on a knack for presenting ideas in writing. Even a well structured report will not get the expected results if it is full of material defects, such as:

- too many pages;
- too much information on the same page;
- lack of titles and sub-titles;
- lines that are too long;
- poor print quality;
- fuzzy (out of register) reproductions;
- hard-to-read text;
- capital letters only; and
- not enough white space around the text.

Reading time should be considered as well. If reading the report takes too much time, the reader probably will not read to the end. The first few pages will be read, and the rest will be skimmed. To ensure a full reading, write a report that can be read in fifteen minutes or less.

HOW TO PROFIT FROM A FAILURE

Despite all efforts, a report may be rejected. It is futile to look for blame. Instead, one should seek the reasons for the rejection by asking:

- Were the ideas presented poorly?
- Was the report too long?
- Were ideas expressed too radically?
- Was there opposition from influential persons?
- Was the timing bad?
- Was credit not given where due?
- Were the proposed changes too costly?
- Did the company not want the benefits?
- Were the observations of the old system incomplete or incorrect?
- Was the information not checked thoroughly?

Among the possible causes of a failure, the analyst can usually find those areas where a better job can be done next time.

CONCLUSION

To present and implement a new or improved system or procedure, a BPI/WS analyst must be able to communicate clearly in both oral and written presentations. One piece of communication that demands skillful verbalization is the analyst's report. Such a report is usually written after a business process is studied and may also present recommendations for process improvement or work simplification.

For an effective report, an analyst must:

- have a striking title for the report;
- communicate his or her message well;
- clearly compare and outline the differences between the old and the new;
- get people involved;
- make decisions easy;
- not promise too much; and
- not offend anyone.

When evaluating his or her report, or even the report of another, an analyst may want to ask the following questions:

- What does each receiver of a report do with the information therein?
- Does the receiver have the authority to act?
- Is the report a duplicate of something else?
- Does it have a control number or does it fall under the jurisdiction of a directive?
- Does the order of the information in the report follow that of the original document?;
- Does the format of the report suit the information needs of the receiver(s)?
- Does the frequency of the report suit the information needs of the receiver(s)?
- Could the report be modified to show exceptions only?

COMPANY MANUALS, POLICIES, AND PROCEDURES

To function effectively, all organizations establish standards for the way they do things. In general, the standards take the form of "policies." The ways of doing things are termed "procedures" or "administrative procedures" or "processes."

ISO 9000
In companies with quality programs already in place, the structure of the ISO series lends itself to augmenting those policies, procedures, and instructions where problems exist or where the risks of failure are greater.

ISO 9000 is a series of quality standards developed by Technical Committee 176 of the International Organization of Standards (ISO). The American National Standards Institute (ANSI), the U.S. member of ISO, states: "There is a strong U.S. and international market trend towards requiring independent organizations (called registrars in the U.S.) to confirm that supplier quality systems meet ISO 9000 requirements (ISO 9000 information fact sheet)."

The series includes the following standards:
- ISO 9001 "Quality systems—Model for quality assurance in design/development, production, installation, and serving";
- ISO 9002 "Quality systems—Model for quality assurance in production and installations"; and
- ISO 9003 "Quality systems—Model for quality assurance in inspection and test."

There are also two guidelines:

- ISO 9000 "Quality management and quality assurance standards"; and
- ISO 9004 "Quality management and quality system elements—Guidelines."

A good reference that features these is *ISO 9000 International Standards for Quality Management*, third edition, which is available from ANSI.

Those who drafted the ISO 9000 planned for a high-level set of quality criteria that, regardless of the size of the company, is worth implementing to some degree or another. The standards are generic and therefore are open to interpretation by various types of businesses. They may be tailored for a single individual selling consulting services or a large, multi-location, high risk, high profile organization making products used by multiple organizations and authorized by a high level executive.

Whether or not they are based on these standards, to make policies and procedures known, companies usually send out directives that are collected in various manuals or guides.

MANUALS AND GUIDES

There are employee guides that deal with conditions of employment, fringe benefits, and union contracts. There are also guides for specialized work groups such as sales personnel and others.

Only two are discussed here: *the organization manual* and the *procedures (processes) manual*. The latter is often called a policies and procedures manual. The preparation and distribution of these manuals are often closely associated with the systems department or BPI/WS department. In cases where this work is the responsibility of the human resources, or personnel, department, a BPI/WS analyst or consultant is often called upon to assist with their revision.

THE ORGANIZATION MANUAL

The organization manual usually is divided into four parts: policies, organization charts, job descriptions (including function guides), and normalized manpower total or authorized establishment (which includes the delegation of authority diagrams).

For each of these parts, there are documents, the contents, composition, and structure of which are dictated by how they are used.

Policies clarify management's point of view on questions dealing with the activities of the company. They also define the latitude given to employees and differ from rules and regulations, which set absolute standards for behavior and offer no latitude whatsoever. Policies often appear as memos.

Organization charts are the graphic representation of a company's structure. They show the company's departments and their hierarchical links. There are two main types: "family tree" and "circular." In the family tree type, the departments of a company follow one another from the top to the bottom of the scale.

In the circular organization chart, the departments of the company are represented by circular segments. The distance between circles is proportionate to the number of hierarchical echelons from the center to the end of the circle. Those with the same hierarchical rank are at the same distance from the center.

Three levels of organization charts may be distinguished, according to their subject:

- the overall organization chart, which broadly represents the main divisions of a company;
- the *divisional organization chart*, which shows the functions and the hierarchical links of a particular section; and
- the *analytical organization chart*, which is a divisional chart with a summarized description of its functions.

Job descriptions enable the identification of structural deficiencies, such as the duplication of responsibilities, that generate conflicts and hinder productivity. They also address a legitimate concern. Workers like to know where they fit into the company and the value of their contribution(s).

Each of the elements of a job description has its importance. The order in which they usually appear on a job description is as follows:

- job title;
- department's name;
- title of immediate supervisor;
- salary scale or salary class;
- summary of the job;
- brief and complete description of each area of activity;
- responsibilities and authority tied to each function;
- contacts to maintain, both internally and externally;
- formal education and training required; and
- experience required.

The *functions guide* is a resume of job descriptions as they fit within the overall activities of the company. Its role is complementary to the overall and departmental organization charts. It limits its content to a summary of the job, a brief description of each area of activity, and of contacts to maintain.

The *normalized total manpower* (authorized establishment) chart tracks various departmental needs. It helps management plan recruiting and, if need be, reassigning personnel. For each department, this chart identifies:

- authorized personnel complement for a given period;
- permanent and temporary personnel complement at the beginning of the period;
- reduction through resignations, terminations, retirements, deaths, and so on;
- permanent and temporary personnel added;
- actual personnel complement at the end of a given period; and
- variance between actual and authorized complement.

A key component of the normalized total manpower chart is the delegation of authority diagram. This useful tool can prevent the conflicts, friction, and poor output caused by duplication or vague definitions. It clarifies the function of each hierarchical level, which eliminates replication and accelerates decision-making. It also shows all the activities of the company under appropriate headings and the corporate level of authority needed for approving those activities.

PREPARATION OF AN ORGANIZATION MANUAL

The preparation of charts and documents that are part of the organization manual calls for scrupulous attention to detail. All aspects must state clearly and without ambiguity management's views. Personal interpretations should be kept to a minimum since many people will be consulting these documents. There is computer software available to help with this.

A representative of senior management must approve the organization manual before publication. Thus, it becomes an official document and cannot be modified according to any one employee's whim.

◆ Modifications and Updates

Company policies continually change under pressure of internal as well as external circumstances. For an organization manual to be useful, it must be updated constantly. For example, accepting suggestions made by BPI/WS analysts may bring about the elimination or complete transformation of certain functions. Organization charts, among others, must be modified to reflect these changes.

Once a year, those who have organization manuals should receive a list of all the documents that should be part of the manual. They can then verify whether their manuals are current, delete outdated documents, and request missing documents.

◆   Distribution

The distribution of an organization manual is the exclusive responsibility of senior management. The analyst must respect instructions and make sure that no one is forgotten.

THE PROCEDURES MANUAL

The procedures manual, or the systems and procedures manual, consists exclusively of work procedures, e.g., information on how to do each task. Its purpose is to guide the work of people. Its main goal is to make the work uniform, no matter who performs it. It is particularly useful for training new employees and refreshing the memories of others temporarily assigned to tasks other than their own.

It is obvious that the analyst writing administrative procedures must have them approved by the department head in question. It would be even better if, before publication, these procedures could receive approval from a member of senior management.

The distribution of the procedures manual follows the same rules as for the organization manual.

ORGANIZATION

A numbering system and an index are usually used to organize a procedures manual. There are several ways to number procedures. The most common is to give a number made up of two elements: first, the number of the department responsible for the task, followed by a number that indicates the order of the procedure.

Take, for example, a traveling expense reimbursement procedure. The finance department is responsible for this procedure. The accounting system has given the finance department the number 603. Consequently, the number should start with 603. Next, will come the order in which the procedure was written within that department, e.g., 14. The procedure number would therefore be 603-14.

Starting from the chosen numbering system, it is preferable to organize the procedures in the manual by department. This organizational tactic is referred to as a numerical filing system.

It is also possible to organize the departments alphabetically and the procedures in each numerically. This is called an alpha-numerical filing system.

An index should always be alphabetical. It should include more than one way to find the required procedure. Procedure 603-14, for example, could be found under any or all of the following:
- expense reimbursement, (traveling);
- reimbursement (traveling expense); or
- traveling (expense reimbursement).

The way to do this is to ask how people would look for a certain procedure and determine several ways of finding it. It is best to have more than one way of locating any procedure.

UPDATING AND MODIFYING

When updating procedures, always reprint a full page at a time. It is therefore essential to put an asterisk (*) or some other sign to indicate the paragraph(s) where modifications have been made.

Procedures are not only changed by an analyst's study. The person doing the task is very often the best person to improve a procedure. In writing or examining a procedures manual, the analyst must take into account this last and very important factor.

A circular letter sent to the manual holders will point out the modifications made to or the elimination of a procedure. Such a circular must indicate required action, such as: "remove procedures titled X and Y issued on. . . ."

The distribution twice a year of a list of procedures the manual should contain ensures that nothing is missing, that all changes have

N°	Issue date	Check, if wanted
603-14	August 3, 1991	
603-15	November 15, 1992	
603-16	September 8, 1993	

FIGURE 8.1 - SAMPLE LIST OF PROCEDURES TO BE INCLUDED IN MANUAL UPDATE PROCESS

been made, and that outdated procedures have been eliminated. This list should include space to order any missing procedure. An example is shown in figure 8.1.

WRITING ADMINISTRATIVE PROCEDURES

The *administrative procedures* describe the activities that a group of people must do. The written account of what one person has to do is called a job description. Administrative procedures are defined in a step-by-step written account of how to do the work.

The objectives of administrative procedures are to:
- indicate clearly to groups of people the activities they must perform;
- coordinate the activities of various groups; and
- help employees and groups of persons work as a team to get the expected results.

All administrative procedures give orders; therefore, all the messages must be clear and precise. Explaining terms and goals or offering opinions and comments may cause confusion.

In other words, adhere to the essentials: a brief statement of the policy to follow and the tasks to be executed, including the sequence in which they are to be done (usually chronologically).

For an administrative procedure to be useful, it must:
- specify who does what when;
- correspond to only one work cycle;
- give each work cycle a logical and precise starting and ending point;
- be presented in two columns: in the left column, the actors (person, group, department); in the right column, the activities;
- describe the activities essential for accomplishing the work;
- connect the activities in a logical order;
- use simple language and short sentences that begin with an action verb, preferably in the present indicative; and
- reserve exceptions, objectives, and explanations for other sections.

To be clear about who-does-what-when, make use of flow charts. If an analyst carefully indicates on his or her flow chart the name of the procedure and the subject studied, the logical work cycle is also established. All that remains is writing the step-by-step procedure. The flow chart should remain with the administrative procedure as a guide to their placement in the overall activities scheme. Even if the procedure identifies the name and number of the form to use, it is useful to attach a copy to the procedure.

THE PLAYSCRIPT TECHNIQUE

A useful method for writing procedures is the *playscript technique,* which describes procedures in the manner of a theatrical script. It was developed because of a number of similarities between the two (Mathies, 1961).

Procedures and theatrical plays have more than one thing in common. Both employ people, actions, and directions to accomplish a certain predetermined result. A script tells each actor what to do; a procedure tells each department, group, or employee the same thing. If a script is not clear about an actor's movements and timing, the play will not communicate the playwright's message. A procedure that is not clear about "what," "who," and "when" will not produce the desired results.

The playscript technique refers to procedures as a work system. Figure 8.2 illustrates a playscript model.

The fundamental aspects of the playscript are as follows:
- it identifies the actors;
- it indicates the action;
- it follows a rigorous chronological order; and
- it represents a complete work cycle.

The actors are the employees or agents involved in each operation.

Actor	Logical Sequence of Operations	Action Word*	Action Sentence
Title	1.	action	. . .
Title	2.	action	. . .
Title	3.	action	. . .
Title	4.	action	. . .
Title	5.	action	. . .

FIGURE 8.2 - A PLAYSCRIPT MODEL

Naming the actors by their titles, never by name, in the left column (see fig. 8.2) determines immediately what jobs are involved and at what level. A job title appears with the first operation to be done, and if it is not repeated, the same person must do each subsequent operation without interruption. A new title only appears where there is a change of actor.

The action in the playscript shows how to proceed. Each step of the work system starts with an action verb in the present indicative tense. (It is a command). A brief sentence then describes what the actor must do. If there is a condition, it must precede the sentence that describes the action. For example: "4. If Form 603-14 is not complete, send it to ..."

In a playscript, the work system's step-by-step procedures are documented in rigorous chronological order. Each step represents a distinct operation. The consecutive numbers that identify the steps indicate the order of the operation. If two operations are done simultaneously, they are shown with indentation and a lower case letter.

For example:
Coding Clerk...
   8. Complete two copies of form 603-14, and
   9. Put:
     a) the routing slip with the first copy, and
     b) the filing slip with the second copy.
   10. Send both copies to the distribution center.

The overall procedure depicts a complete work cycle. To be complete, the work procedure must include the beginning, the main steps, and the end of the work cycle.

In theory, a work cycle may have nine steps or nine hundred. Experience has shown, however, that the shorter procedures are the most efficient if they are complete.

The best way to limit the length of a procedure is to include in the work procedure only information concerning what must be done and exclude the reasons for doing certain tasks. Then, briefly show the reasons why the procedure exists under the heading of "Subject."

If longer explanations seem necessary, put them in a separate preamble, or in an introductory chapter in the procedures manual.

The following is an example of how the playscript technique clarifies and simplifies documentation of a work system.

◆   Document 1

Subject: Transfers and adjustment of the personnel budget.

The Company policy and adopted practices make provisions for the transfer of employees from one department to another as the need arises.

Personnel transfers cannot be done without adjusting the budgets and the work expenditure registers beforehand, usually kept by the Accounting and Finance Division, Budget and Planning section.

In the case of transfers from an administrative department to operations, the Personnel Department will have the necessary authority to ask for the signature of the different Department Supervisors where the employees will be transferred. The Personnel Department will set the official transfer date which will be entered on Form 457, "Transfer Request," in the space provided. Copies 2 and 3 will be sent to the receiving department while copy 1 will be kept on file in the transferring department.

The respective budgets and Work Expenditure registers are adjusted as per Form 457 which will be sent to the Budget and Planning Section of the Accounting and Finance Department.

The transfer request is not effective without the preliminary approval of the transferring department supervisor and that of the receiving department as well.

The employee's file, different from that in the Personnel department, will be sent to the receiving department at the same time as Form 457. All other documents affected by the transfer will be modified to indicate the transfer, notably for the receiving department since the files of the receiving department must be kept up-to-date and each employee must be charged against the proper expense account.

The Company policy is to keep the employees' files in a locked Personnel filing cabinet. Only supervisors have access to these files, and only they have the right to consult them.

Document 1 is an example of an administrative procedure description found in numerous companies. Apparently its author knew the procedure and understood it. But does this procedure tell the user how to proceed with transfers? Can it be determined:

  • where and how the procedure starts;

- where it ends; and
- who does what and when?

Would a supervisor know how to ask for a transfer of personnel, or how to do one?

Companies with such confusing and ambiguous documentation often compile abstracts and consult an "expert" (i.e., the supervisor of the human resources department) for directives on how to go about it. When experienced personnel are allowed to interpret, the procedure in Document 1 can produce positive results despite the shortcomings of the documentation. However, what would happen if a new supervisor asked a new human resources supervisor for directives and/or clarifications?

Procedures exist, above all, for new employees and for experienced employees called upon to carry out tasks they rarely do (such as transferring an employee). To be effective, the documentation must show each person having to do a job, what has to be done and when it has to be done. If those points are not set out in a clear and simple manner, there will be numerous misunderstandings and errors. Some people will even completely ignore the written procedure and call on an "expert."

Document 1 sets out a work system in a clumsy and confusing way. This is not due to the writer's lack of knowledge. Instead, it lacks the appropriate means of conveying the necessary knowledge to users.

Document 2, which follows, describes the same procedure as Document 1, but in the playscript fashion.

◆   **Document 2**

Subject: Personnel transfers—Steps to follow

Policy: Employees will be transferred from one department to another according to department needs.

Person responsible	*Measures to be taken*
Receiving Supervisor	1. Complete Form 457, "Transfer Request" for additional personnel.
	2. Send all copies of the form to the Human Resources Supervisor.
Human Resources Supervisor	3. Recruit the employee to be transferred.
	4. Set the transfer date.
	5. Get verbal approval (for the

employee and the transfer date) from both transferring and receiving supervisors.

6. Enter the employee's name and the date of transfer on all copies of the Transfer Request.
7. Enter the change in the employee's file kept in the Human Resources Department.
8. Put copy 1 of the Transfer Request in the file kept by the Human Resources Department.
9. File it in the Human Resources Department files.
10. Send Copies 2 and 3 to the Budget and Planning Section Supervisor.

Supervisor,
Budget and Planning

11. Make the necessary adjustments to the budget and work charges registers.
12. Send the two copies of the Transfer Request to the Transferring Supervisor.

Supervisor, Transferring

13. Enter the change in the department register
14. Advise the employee of his transfer.
15. Send the employee's file and the two copies of the transfer request to the receiving supervisor.

Supervisor, Receiving

16. Enter the change in the department's register.
17. Put the employee's file and copy 2 of the transfer request in the locked Human Resources filing cabinet.
18. Sign copy 3 and send it to the Human Resources Supervisor.

Human Resources Supervisor

19. Put copy 3 in the Human Resources Department files.

End of operations

Document 2 tells the user how to proceed for the transfer of an employee. In other words, it indicates:
- where and how the procedure starts;
- all the persons using the procedure and the measures each one has to apply;
- the order in which the operations must take place; and
- where and how the procedure ends.

The playscript forces the writer to take into account these four key points. Moreover, it offers numerous other possibilities.

PLAYSCRIPT SUB-PROCEDURES

A procedure that is likely to be long and complex because it includes all the aspects of a work cycle should be divided. First, there should be an explanation of the normal flow of operations (or the most frequent operations). Then, sub-procedures should be detailed that deal with:
- exceptions to the normal flow (correcting errors);
- the most frequent tasks; and
- the detailed execution of tasks that are the responsibility of only a select group.

The presence of a certain number of elements is necessary for the normal flow of most procedures. An example is receiving a properly completed and signed request or properly coded form. If one of these elements is missing (if, for example, the request received is not signed), a sub-procedure must provide for this. There are two ways to present a sub-procedure. If the sub-procedure is simple and short (less than ten steps), indent it in the procedure and identify the different steps with a small letter. For example:

Clerk X   9. Check coding on form 603-14 to ensure accuracy.
              10. If there is an error,
                  a) underline the coding error;
                  b) complete routing slip, etc.
              11. Send form 603-14 to Data Entry

In the above example, only the accurate data goes to step 11 (normal flow of the procedure).

If the sub-procedure is complex or long, write it separately and reference it. For example:

Clerk X	9. Check coding on form 603-14 to ensure accuracy.
	10. If there is an error, refer to step 09.15, "Sub-procedure in case of error."
	11. Send form 603-14 to Data Entry

Here again, only the accurate data goes to step 11 (normal flow of procedure).

◆   **Playscript Interactive Procedure**
The playscript technique makes provision for only one actor at a time. Therefore, in the case of a multiple-copy form, the handling of which involves an interaction, it may be difficult to write about the procedure.

Here is how to ensure continuity, using "refer to":

Clerk A	5. Complete form 603.14.
	6. Put copy 1 of form 603.14 in file X and file it away.
	7. Separate the other copies of form 603.14, and a) send copy 3 to Clerk C (see step 11). b) send copy 2 to Clerk B.
Clerk B	8. Do this.
	9. Do that.
	10. Put copy 2 in file Y and put it away (end of operations for Clerk B).
Clerk C	11. Upon receiving copy 3 of form 603.14, remove file Z from filing cabinet.
	12. Do this.

CONCLUSION

BPI/WS analysts and consultants are often called upon to evaluate and even revise a company's organization manual and procedure manual. Procedure manuals are particularly key. Writing administrative procedures may seem difficult at first, but if the playscript technique is used, procedure manuals will be clear and effective.

A BPI/WS analyst or consultant should remember the following when drafting a procedures manual:

- wear the users' shoes. Procedures can be a useless burden for those who have no need to know them;
- write short procedures. Use sub-procedures to lighten the

text. There are two kinds of sub-procedures; those kept within the main text and those referred to separately;

- if they are really necessary, include comments on objectives, opinions, and policies. But keep them separate. Procedures that are too long or that give too much information will only confuse the user, who will be unable to identify the few crucial items;
- use clear and direct language;
- use "action" verbs and terms that tell the user exactly what to do;
- use the present indicative tense, not the future. The person reading a procedure usually must do the job as he or she reads; and
- give positive instructions. Tell the user what to do, rather than what not to do. For example, instead of "long-distance telephone calls should not be done without the Supervisor's prior authorization," say "get the Supervisor's authorization before making a long-distance telephone call."

OFFICE LAYOUT

A BPI/WS analyst and/or team member should be familiar with office arrangement and layout, for he or she may be asked to examine proposals from firms specializing in this area. He or she may have to evaluate the arrangements or layouts made by others. Therefore, an analyst should know, firsthand, about the space necessary for each department.

Office arrangement and layout have two characteristic components: the arrangement of the desks and equipment necessary for the work to be done in a given area, and the allocation of space that allows maximum productivity at minimum cost. In other words, office arrangement should aim first and foremost at efficiency and economy (Contant, 1972).

SPACE ALLOCATION

A general examination of the work area also allows an analyst to propose better utilization of the space available. For example, the stronger floors should be used for heavy equipment, the areas around the elevators for public interaction, and fireproof areas for archives and permanent records.

Allocation of space varies according to the disposition of the building's services, the standards for the furniture and the private offices, the spacing of windows and walls, the size and divisions of departments, and the nature of the company's work itself. The current needs of the departments, as well as future needs, are important. Normal expansion should be considered.

Space requirements are usually established from recognized standards. Most companies have standards that range from 60 square feet for clerks to 100 square feet for higher-level employees to as much as 400 square feet for executives. Canadian and U.S. standards are a minimum of 70 square feet per person.

OFFICES

Large open areas with private offices separated by movable partitions offer the maximum flexibility. The departments can then expand or contract as the need arises without great cost.

Hierarchical levels and job requirements determine the characteristics for private offices: their size, the height of the partitions, whether the floor is carpeted, the style and cost of desk, chairs, credenzas, drapes, and so forth. Private offices are generally reserved for senior personnel (officers and senior management), personnel dedicated to research and study projects, and those who deal in confidential matters. They are also sometimes given to individuals for reasons of prestige.

It is a good idea to plan for private offices and a few well-equipped study/meeting/conference rooms for workers to use occasionally.

WORKSTATIONS

A workstation represents not only where a worker conducts professional activities but also where the majority of his or her active life is spent. The following factors are therefore important:
- the physiological and psychological needs of the worker (ambiance, physical necessities, and so forth);
- the requirements of the work, i.e., the space for the equipment and documentation needed for work flow, and the rational utilization of space;
- the contacts outside the work area, such as personnel movements and communications with the public; and
- the worker's role and responsibilities, the importance of his or her functions, and his or her rank in the hierarchy.

FURNITURE

Work requirements determine the quality of the worker's furniture, the size of the desks, the number of side tables, and other such needs. The worker's rank also comes into consideration.

Despite variations due to hierarchical rank, each worker must be supplied with the furniture necessary for performing assigned functions.

DESKS AND CHAIRS

Desks are all generally the same height. For the worker to be comfortable, his or her arms must rest on the desk when he or she is seated. It is preferable to choose chairs with adjustable seats and backs. For comfort, feet should touch the ground, the back be positioned at the back of the chair, and legs should be in a horizontal position.

THE ENVIRONMENT (AMBIANCE)

Environment influences the workers' output. It can stimulate, distract, or crush. A detailed study of the environment requires knowledge possessed only by specialists. However, there are a few characteristics that any analyst may take into consideration.

LIGHTING

Lighting must be well-distributed, sufficient, and intense enough to allow work to be done. Good lighting helps prevent accidents and fatigue. In general, light must be uniform and come from the left, parallel with the line of vision.

Different levels of lighting are necessary for various tasks. It is best to rely on specialists for help in this area. Relying on expert advice for guidelines to minimize the problems of individuals working in front of terminals, computers, or word processors is best. However, there are a few rules that apply to most workplaces.

Natural lighting is preferable to artificial lighting. It is almost always necessary to regulate the flow of light with blinds to prevent glare.

Clean windows and lighting equipment are important. Dirt greatly diminishes the flow, quality, and quantity of light. Fluorescent tubes should be washed at least annually.

It is best to try to avoid arranging people so that they face windows or so that their backs are to a window. Facing the window will affect their eyesight (it is tiresome for the eyes to face a light source for a long period). When their backs are to the window, a shadow will be thrown on their work. The light may also blind their visitors. If a worker faces a wall, his or her desk (or work station) should be at least 20 feet from the wall so his or her field of vision varies.

HEATING, VENTILATION, AND AIR CONDITIONING

Temperatures that are too high or too low and inadequate ventilation reduce workplace productivity and vitality. In general, the temperature should be maintained around 70 degrees Fahrenheit (21 degrees

Celsius) and the relative humidity between 40 and 50 percent. Good air circulation and periodic exchange of the building's air with outside environment are strongly recommended. Computer rooms should have their own special air conditioning and ventilation systems.

SOUNDPROOFING

Noise does not bother some people. Experience shows, however, that it often causes fatigue and irritation. In an office, the noise level should not go beyond 30 decibels. A good way to reduce noise, is to contain it at its source, with soundproofing material, covers, carpets under noise producing machines, and periodic maintenance and lubrication of equipment.

HOW TO PROCEED

Rarely does an analyst supervise the arrangement and layout of new offices. His or her work is more likely to be the rearrangement of existing offices. In such a case, the best way to tackle the problem is to use the existing plan and a plan of the space available.

Before proceeding, one should always verify that the plans supplied match the actual space. Modifications often occur during construction that are not recorded on the original plans. Whenever possible, visit the site to compare the plans with reality.

EXISTING LAYOUT

Use the existing layout to note the location of:
- equipment and the furniture for an inventory of the material to be discarded. There is no point in rearranging things that are no longer necessary or useful;
- special needs such as storage space, telephone room, soundproofed meeting rooms, private offices, and so on;
- the work flow and traffic aisles. There are, sometimes, more than one flow of work in a given section. In that case, chart one flow superimposed on another to achieve an acceptable compromise. To establish the volume of traffic, take into account the needs in ordinary circumstances, those in peak periods and those in case of an emergency, such as personnel arrival and departure times, and evacuation. Use dotted lines and arrows to show the activity in the section to rearrange (fig. 9.1); and
- the name, functions, and hierarchical level of each worker.

SPACE AVAILABLE

On the plan of the space available, the analyst should indicate the dimensions, building characteristics, and the limits to its use. The accuracy of the plan and whether it is to scale should be verified. All missing information such as the thickness and location of columns, should be entered.

Permanent fixtures—stairs, passages, rest rooms, and elevators—should be shown first. Then, the analyst should identify the movable elements—partitions, electrical outlets, and telephone jacks.

The building's limits include the load capacity of the floors, areas where holes may not be created, and the location of electrical ducts.

THE PROPOSED PLAN

An analyst must present the broad lines of the proposed rearrangement to management and secure management's suggestions. He or she should also point out:
- the shortcomings of the present arrangement, what the workers think of it, and the proposed correction(s);
- the physiological and psychological factors that can affect the arrangement (disabled persons or incompatibility of character); and
- the plans for the future, such as increasing or decreasing equipment and staff.

Draw up the proposed plan according to the accepted standards, the possibilities and limits of the floor plans, and personal observations. Start with the departments and workers who must, because of their work and the building's characteristics, occupy a predetermined place in the building. Determine the location of the other departments according to the flow diagram (see fig. 9.1).

When positioning offices, it is customary to respect certain practices:
- when the situation permits, offices for the same level of employees should be positioned and spaced identically. The offices of those who manage employees should be arranged so that these managers can see most activities for which they are responsible;
- if possible, locate employees according to hierarchical importance. Similarly, position the department according to its importance to senior management; and
- offer choice space (corners, windows, near the windows, and so forth) to the most important employees.

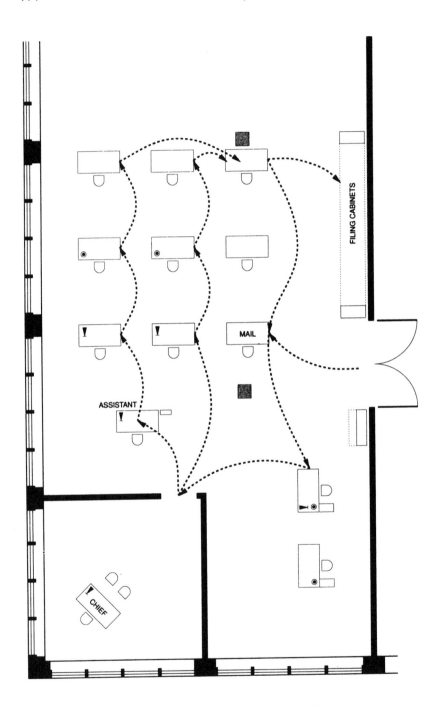

FIGURE 9.1 - OPERATIONS FLOW DIAGRAM

To ensure discipline and the well-being of the workers, take into account the following factors:

- the arrangement of large, open offices should allow for a rational use of space, while putting too many people in a given space creates fatigue; and
- it also is wise to separate people that share a common work flow using partitions, a series of file cabinets, or offices.

The drawing of the plan should be done in a systematic fashion. Computer software is available that can be used in this process.

Private offices, aisles, partitions, and other separations should be drawn first; then, use templates or patterns to position the desks, chairs, and equipment. The employee's name and telephone number should appear on each desk. Electrical outlets and telephone jacks should be shown next. Finally, indicate the location of directional signs (emergency exits, door numbers, the department name, and private offices).

Once the first draft of the plan has been drawn, its designer should present it to the departments concerned and those responsible for its implementation. If necessary, the plan may be revised and then approved by the departments concerned. Then, the designer should prepare a final copy and reproduce in sufficient copies for all concerned.

MOVING

The rearrangement of offices often coincides with a move to other, possibly new, quarters. A few hints on that subject are:

- make a complete inventory of the furniture, equipment and supplies;
- set a moving date that allows the completion of technical rearrangements in the new location;
- arrange for the move to take place outside normal working hours;
- put a sticker on each piece of furniture and equipment with a number indicating the destination—floor and room;
- number each employee's furniture and equipment and put that number on the copy of the plan given to the movers;
- accept the mover's suggestions for the contents of desks and filing equipment;
- give each worker a notebook showing their new work station and provide a list of new telephone numbers;
- station workers at both the old and new locations to monitor the move and ensure everything reaches its proper place;

- make sure that everything has been moved, including what was on the walls and in private and closed offices;
- if anything is damaged or broken, bring it to the movers' attention immediately; and
- make sure all the mover's employees have proper identification to prevent possible theft.

CONCLUSION

A BPI/WS analyst rarely designs office facilities; however, he or she can make recommendations for office layout as it relates to simplifying and improving business processes. The general information discussed in this chapter should help analysts and consultants review, evaluate, and revise current office layouts.

STRUCTURE OF THE
BPI/WS FUNCTION

The BPI/WS department is basically a reactive operation that responds to either a request from a department or a directive from senior management.

Any department can request that the BPI/WS department study a recurring departmental problem and recommend solutions. In such cases, the analyst's mandate is clear and precise. The cooperation of the requesting department is assured.

From reports received, senior management often detects inefficiencies in one or more departments. At the same time, the department heads concerned maintain that their workers are doing a good job. In these situations, senior management often asks the BPI/WS department to study the situation and propose effective remedial action(s). In such cases, not surprisingly, the analyst may encounter a defensive attitude from the department personnel in question. This is perhaps the supreme test of consulting abilities. The experienced analyst succeeds by using tact and diplomacy while gathering facts and suggesting solutions.

BPI/WS analysts must always remember that their department has an auxiliary role, that of consultant. The BPI/WS department has no direct authority over any other department(s).

CENTRALIZED AND DECENTRALIZED STRUCTURES

Many experts have noted the tendency for organizational structure to be cyclical: centralized, decentralized, centralized, and so on—not unlike the movement of a pendulum. BPI/WS has not escaped this trend.

Broadly speaking, *decentralized departments* report to the management of a branch office or a subsidiary. In a *centralized operation*, all units report to the head office. In both cases, one principle is the same: the BPI/WS analyst reports to either the CEO at the head office or the CEO of a decentralized organization's branch office.

Currently, there seems to be a swing toward decentralization, with the BPI/WS function imbedded in operating departments. Whether centralized or decentralized, however, the need for such a function persists. Sometimes an analyst or industrial engineer is found as part of a focused office or factory (administration) team and responsible for a work group.

Since different organizations are in different parts of the cycle, the following is presented as a model appropriate for work simplification where the function exists as a separate department.

To reiterate briefly the discussion in Chapter 2, the role of BPI/WS analysts is: to advise a company of the best ways to use its physical, human, and information resources to improve efficiency and reduce costs.

An effective team of analysts does exactly that. Thus, it should be no surprise when senior management decides to create or reorganize such a group.

BPI/WS PLACEMENT

Senior management must decide where a BPI/WS analyst or group should be located in the company structure and then support that analyst or group, especially one that has been newly created. These

---

Initially, with the team of BPI/WS analysts/consultants:

- Decide on its place within the organization

- Set out its objectives and scope of activities

Then, without fail:

- Give the BPI/WS group all the necessary possible support.

FIGURE 10.1 - RESPONSIBILITIES OF SENIOR MANAGEMENT

responsibilities are clarified in figure 10.1. The analyst or group should, in turn, report to senior management.

If senior management wishes its organization to follow and adhere to its policies, those policies must be well understood and applied. That is another reason there must be a close link between the BPI/WS group and senior management. Additionally, a high level BPI/WS department will be in a better position to resist the pressures others will want to place upon it. In short, the BPI/WS department should report to the person upon whom the president or general manager relies for the broad general administration of the company.

SIZE AND STRUCTURE OF A BPI/WS DEPARTMENT

The size and structure of a BPI/WS department depend on the nature and the scope of its assignments. They should not be tied to the number of employees in the company; rather, size and structure should be linked to the volume and the complexity of the company's activities.

The degree of centralization or decentralization within the company will also affect the size and structure of the group. In small and mid-sized companies, a centralized BPI/WS department is most beneficial. As part of the head office, the BPI/WS personnel are close to the decision-makers in matters concerning policies and project planning. Such an arrangement results in a better overall view of the company's needs. Thanks to the varied experience of its employees, it can rapidly counsel senior management on problems and offer high quality service.

In large companies, the divisions or subsidiaries separated from the head office often complain, not without reason, that a centralized BPI/WS department does not always understand the nuances of local problems. Thus, they think it is incapable of producing valid solutions for them. In these cases, a decentralized function may be a better solution. Another solution is to create regional BPI/WS functions with a team of analysts reporting to a regional BPI/WS department. This department provides the regional departments with analysts and ensures their rotation. It may even send specialized analysts to deal with problems endemic to the region. However, they also report to the central BPI/WS manager about work methods, equipment standards, and senior management's policies.

For a fairly large department, the following structure is recommended: one manager and three unit managers. Normally, each unit manager heads a specialized group. The first group is responsible for systems analysis. Its members could include a senior analyst, one or more experienced analysts, one or more trainee analysts, and a procedure writer.

The second group handles equipment and space analysis. Its makeup is like the first without the procedure writer. The third group analyzes forms. It could consist of a senior analyst, a forms or draft person, and a photocomposition operator. An example of an organization chart for this structure is illustrated in figure 10.2.

Naturally, many BPI/WS departments are not organized this way. Analysts have a tendency to specialize. For example, when a project requires a specific background, the responsibility will be given to the person most familiar with the subject in question. The project manager

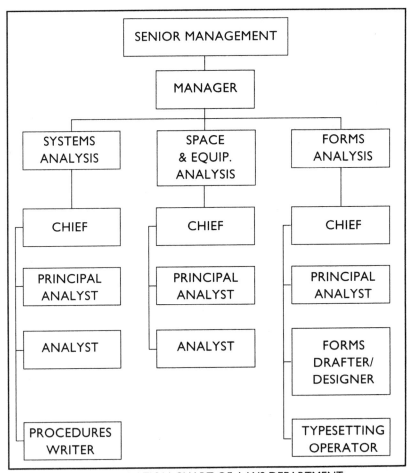

FIGURE 10.2 - ORGANIZATION CHART OF A WS DEPARTMENT

allocates the teams and the tasks according to each individual's specialty and expertise.

CONCLUSION

This chapter has established the fact that a BPI/WS analyst or department's place in a company is determined by its senior management, and that the analyst or department should answer directly to them. If more than one analyst is used, either as a group or department, the size of the company determines whether that group or department is centralized or decentralized. Whether centralized or decentralized, large or small, however, the fact remains that most companies, at one point or another, find that they need BPI/WS. How the function is implemented largely depends on the nature of the company and its systems.

To assist them, BPI/WS analysts should acquire the training and knowledge necessary to understand each company's special needs. That is the subject of the next chapter.

PROFESSIONAL TRAINING

The BPI/WS analyst's "trade" is mostly exercised in an office—an environment that is constantly and rapidly evolving. Today, the office and its activities represent the fastest growth sector of the world economy, yet office automation is far from complete. There will be significant leaps forward in the years to come. An analyst must have an open mind to adapt to the future stages of an integrated office. He or she needs to study and learn continually to keep abreast of innovations.

KNOWLEDGE NECESSARY FOR ANALYSTS

The knowledge necessary for a good analyst is not limited to theory. To the principles of organization and work simplification, one adds the workings of the office, knowledge of equipment and its use, office supplies, forms, and software—as well as theoretical and practical knowledge of personnel training and development. Figure 11.1 summarizes these needs.

There also are specialties in a BPI/WS department. Each requires thorough training for anyone wishing to excel in it. After acquiring basic BPI/WS knowledge, it is always possible to attain competence in these specialties by working with an expert in the particular field.

HOW TO GET TRAINING

On-the-job training is the most useful (even for someone with a truckload of diplomas and certificates). There is a drawback to this kind of training, however. An analyst may become too limited and perhaps difficult to transfer.

Professional associations, such as the Institute of Industrial Engineers (IIE), the American Records Managers Association (ARMA), the Association for Systems Management (ASM), organize very good courses, conferences, and seminars. They are conducted by knowledgeable people with solid, real-world experience. Association meetings are also occasions for fruitful exchanges and for cultivating valuable networks and friendships that last for years.

Each year, new books are published that are of interest for a BPI/WS analyst. Watch particularly for reprints of some of the classic WS works. (See the bibliography.) Reference works may be borrowed from public or private libraries, from many company libraries or, if one is particularly fortunate, from a specialized library.

Many colleges and universities offer evening courses in administration. Some universities also offer degrees or certificates in business administration. Many companies and organizations offer their employees assistance or partial assistance with tuition. Management consulting firms, specializing in reengineering or work simplification (such as the Ben Graham Corporation), also have courses they can adapt to the needs of customers.

---

1. Practical knowledge of organization and work simplification

2. Practical knowledge of office work

3. Technical knowledge of:

    • equipment

    • office supplies

    • forms

    • software

4. Theoretical and practical knowledge of personnel training and development

---

FIGURE 11.1 - NECESSARY KNOWLEDGE FOR ANALYSTS

Television is also a useful educational resource. A number of stations offer courses and conferences worthy of attention.

CONCLUSION

The growth of office work represents enormous career possibilities for those analysts who take the time to acquire the necessary training and knowledge. Periodic recessions have not halted this expansion. The services of analysts are required more than ever. Why? Because all analysts are dedicated to improving the efficiency and increasing the productivity of their organizations.

A DETAILED INTERVENTION METHODOLOGY AND REVIEW

When the six steps of work simplification identified in Chapter 5 are combined with the other principles and methods discussed in this book, a detailed intervention methodology for a BPI/WS department can be developed.

All studies, whether of manual systems or as a prelude to mechanization, are made up of five stages divided into twenty-three steps. These are illustrated in figure 12.1. Each is discussed below, followed by a summary of the study's key components: meetings, interviews, reports, and documents.

STAGE A: INITIAL STUDY
STEP ONE: MEETING WITH THE SPONSOR
Upon receiving a written request from a department head, a meeting should be planned within five working days.

STEP TWO: REQUEST DEFINITION
The purpose of the meeting is to clarify the request so that the nature, scope, and objectives of the study are defined. The requesting manager must be involved. The minutes of the meeting and additional notes help establish the mandate given the analyst responsible for the study.

A mandate can originate from three sources. The first is the company's corporate plan already approved by senior management. Requests from department heads are the second source. To be acceptable, such mandates must help managers manage better, improve productivity, reduce operating costs, improve controls, and/or promote corporate

STAGES	STEPS
A. Initial Study	1. Meeting with the sponsor
	2. Request definition
	3. Request evaluation
	4. Priority setting
	5. Initial report
B. Preliminary Study	6. Planning
	7. Study of present system
	8. Problem identification
	9. Setting objective(s)
	10. Development of alternative solutions
	11. Cost/benefit comparison
	12. Recommendation(s)
	13. Feasibility report
C. Preparation for implementation	14. Forms specifications
	15. Forms preparation
	16. Procedure specification
	17. Procedure writing
	18. Training preparation
D. Implementation	19. Training
	20. Setting the stage
	21. Final report
E. Follow-up	22. Audit and evaluation
	23. Follow-up report

FIGURE 12.1 - STEP-BY-STEP PROCEDURE FOR COMPLETING A STUDY

policies. Finally, special requests from vice-presidents or senior management constitute the third and last source of possible mandates. The scope of the mandate varies according to the objectives.

Anticipated objectives must be clear and specific. They will orient the work of the team. The final report will show to what extent they have been reached.

From the mandate and the objectives, a provisional estimate of the resources required and time necessary for the conduct of the study can be made. Employees affected should be advised that current estimates of time and resources are only provisional and may change.

STEP THREE: EVALUATING THE REQUEST

The decision to proceed with a computerization study or with a revision of management activities rests with the BPI/WS department manager. The main factors to consider are the origin of the request and the importance of the situation.

The importance of a request should be evaluated against the following criteria. Will it:
- increase profitability?
- promote established policies?
- improve controls?
- facilitate effective management?
- reduce costs?

STEP FOUR: SETTING PRIORITIES

From the information gathered, the BPI/WS department manager sets the relative priority of the mandate and determines the probable date for the start of the study. This priority and probable date are influenced by the following factors:
- the urgency of the situation;
- the availability of analysts;
- the time available in the annual activity plan;
- the availability of the manager(s) affected;
- the availability of qualified specialists; and
- other changes planned or implemented in the affected area.

STEP FIVE: INITIAL REPORT

The initial report formulates recommendations as to whether proceeding with the project is advisable, and if so, suggests a possible starting date. When a decision has been made and a starting date has been set, it is important to put in writing the terms of the mandate. This avoids any later misunderstanding.

The following elements should be entered:
- a brief description of the objectives;
- the nature and scope of the mandate;
- the affected department's contribution;
- the analyst responsible;
- the manager responsible for the case; and
- the expected date for the submission of the preliminary study report.

Any subsequent modification to the mandate must be a written and signed agreement.

STAGE B: PRELIMINARY STUDY

The preliminary study is divided into eight steps that begin with the planning of the study itself.

STEP SIX: PLANNING

In order to plan the execution of a mandate correctly and give an account of the time spent, it is essential to budget time for each step of the study.

The hours needed are estimated roughly so that the unit head will have an idea of the scope of the project. The budget is revised in detail when preparing the action plan for the plan's subsequent steps.

After preparing the time budget in person/days, multiply it by a conversion factor that permits setting the project timetable. This factor takes into account time not spent on the project (other projects, holidays, official holidays, sick days, and others). The rate may be revised from time to time, according to circumstances. Note that this timetable must take into account the date set for the final report in the initial study report. The planning is then plotted on a Gantt chart to be used for control purposes throughout the project.

STEP SEVEN: STUDY OF THE PRESENT SYSTEM

This step is the description of the present situation or system. Flow charts and other tools described in Chapter 5 should be used.

A description of the current situation should answer the following questions:
- How does the work flow?
- What parts cannot be modified for legal or other reasons?

- What forms exist?
- Which forms are used?
- Who completes the forms and how?
- What are the procedures?
- What is the present equipment?
- How efficient is the equipment?
- To what extent is the equipment used?
- Is the equipment sufficient and adequate?
- What standards are used and which are not used?
- Who authorized these standards and when?
- How is the work distributed between the workers?
- What are each worker's responsibilities?

STEP EIGHT: PROBLEM IDENTIFICATION

Once the current situation is described, the analyst can evaluate the situation and identify the problem(s) to correct. These problems usually fall into two categories. First, there are the problems inherent in the present system. Consider:
- volume;
- deadlines;
- costs; and
- quality.

Then there are the present costs. Consider the costs of:
manpower (salaries);
- forms;
- delays;
- rush jobs; and
- equipment and machines.

A detailed examination is used to gather and analyze the information necessary to reach the project objectives. To do this, an analyst must:
- assure that all the data gathered in the preceding steps has been arranged methodically and that its pertinence has been considered;
- analyze the data using the appropriate techniques;
- compare the data with the reference criteria; and
- assess the information, i.e., evaluate its adequacy, pertinence, and reliability as well as the effectiveness of the controls.

The accuracy of verbal or written information or data obtained is crucial. It would be counterproductive to have the results of the analysis questioned. The data file must be complete, legible, and adequately identified. Departmental managers' comments may be used as data and entered in the file. They must, however, be used with discretion, for they often represent opinions and not obvious facts.

STEP NINE: SETTING THE OBJECTIVE(S)

To set the objective(s) for the new system or new work organization, the following should be considered:

- What are the strengths of the present situation?
- What are the weaknesses of the present situation?
- What objectives should be aimed for?
- What should be accomplished in terms of:
    -controls,
    -cost reduction,
    -utilization of strengths,
    -elimination of weaknesses, and
    -increased productivity?

STEP TEN: DEVELOPMENT OF ALTERNATIVE SOLUTIONS

Possible solutions answer the objectives and are then developed with new flow charts.

Examples of possible solutions are:

- abolition;
- mechanization:
    -partial,
    -total, or
    -none;
- computer versus manual systems;
- change(s) in structure;
- modification of the work distribution; and
- modification or establishment of standards.

STEP ELEVEN: COSTS AND BENEFITS COMPARISON

Each solution will need a separate evaluation and a comparison of costs and benefits. From these, it can be decided which would be more profitable for the company. Two basic questions are involved:

- Which one(s) should be kept and why?
- Which is the best solution and why?

STEP TWELVE: RECOMMENDATION(S)

After the analysis, choose one or more recommendation(s) and offer it or them to the requesting department.

STEP THIRTEEN: FEASIBILITY REPORT

A *feasibility report* for implementing the results of the preliminary study is then prepared and submitted to management. This involves a preliminary study report and a presentation of the recommendations.

◆   Preliminary Study Report

While writing the preliminary study report, the analyst should adhere to the following:
- describe facts accurately;
- be brief and concise;
- present the main points well;
- use language the reader can understand;
- be tactful and keep a positive attitude in the text;
- present logical conclusions and recommendations; and
- formulate practical and feasible recommendations.

◆   Presenting the Recommendations

The goal is to discuss the recommendations so that they will approved and acted upon immediately. To prepare, the analyst must organize a meeting (date, place, time) and invite everyone directly affected by the recommendations. Those indirectly affected by the recommendations could also be present. Before the presentation, the analyst should organize his or her notes so that he or she can easily answer any question that might arise.

For the actual presentation, an audiovisual presentation offers many advantages:
- it forces the analyst to prepare a complete summary of the essentials;
- it keeps everyone's attention on the same material;
- it eliminates having to read pages of text; and
- it makes decisions easier.

The importance of the report will demonstrate the necessity of such a presentation. As much as possible, the analyst should promote user participation. For example, users can give superior explanations because of direct involvement in the area. Furthermore, the recommendation presented is often a user's idea.

Minutes of the meeting must be prepared and sent to everyone present. They will indicate the decisions made and the dates for implementing them.

STAGE C: PREPARING FOR IMPLEMENTATION

Once the decision is made to implement the recommendation(s), preparations must be made to do so.

STEP FOURTEEN: FORMS SPECIFICATION

To define the specifications for forms necessary for the new or amended system, evaluate the forms currently used by:
- reviewing the data that appears on more than one form each time certain transactions are made;
- justifying the existence of all forms and identifying where improvements could be made;
- reviewing the usefulness of the data entered on the form to see if it would be possible to preprint some or change the place where it is entered on the form;
- comparing possible improvement of the form;
- evaluating the cost and possible savings of typing or word processing the form(s); and
- evaluating the cost and of possible savings of printing the form(s).

STEP FIFTEEN: PREPARING THE FORMS

Chapter 6 discusses how to prepare the specified forms at length.

STEPS SIXTEEN AND SEVENTEEN: SPECIFYING AND WRITING THE PROCEDURES

The specifications for the manual procedures are analyzed and written from the new or amended system's flow charts according to the writing standards in Chapter 7.

STEP EIGHTEEN: TRAINING PREPARATION

The training necessary for new or changed systems is designed based on the written procedures.

STAGE D: IMPLEMENTATION

The affected department management ensures the implementation of the new or amended system with the analyst as advisor. The analyst prepares an implementation program with the unit manager who announces it to the staff, and a responsible manager holds a meeting with the employees. This meeting announces the coming changes, the goals to reach, and the implementation plan. All ambiguous situations may then be clarified. Note is also taken of all remarks and comments from the employees. The publication of this program is an important part in the success of the project.

The existing computer applications at the time of the study may introduce some constraints in the form of necessary modifications. The new applications may also bring their own constraints: choice and delivery of equipment and software, familiarization, running both systems in parallel, and so forth. These elements and the delays they cause must be taken into consideration when preparing the implementation timetable.

When preparing the timetable, consider also the staff's workload, hiring and training problems, budget restrictions, and time constraints. Similarly, be cautious with the length of the timetable. An analyst does not want to lose the staff's interest. Implementation that takes too much time often causes negative reactions as well.

Step Nineteen: Training
The employees affected by the new system must be trained in the new way of doing things.

Step Twenty: Setting the Stage
The preparations for all the necessary changes for the new situation include:
- rewriting and modifying job descriptions and having them approved;
- ensuring the learning of the new procedures; and
- reviewing space allocation;

Adequate supervision must be exercised throughout this step to answer questions from the affected employees and to settle problems as they occur.

During this step, the information and entries made and processed in the new system are reviewed to make sure that the system will produce the expected results. An analyst may then have to revise and/or adapt corrective measures to the new systems. Running both the old and new systems for a predetermined period may be helpful.

STEP TWENTY-ONE: THE FINAL REPORT

The final report should confirm the adoption or acceptance of the new system. The date of the eventual follow-up and control steps are also set in the final report.

STAGE E: FOLLOW-UP
STEP TWENTY-TWO: AUDIT AND EVALUATION

After the final report has been submitted, the analyst performs a detailed audit and evaluation of the new system or new situation. Answers to the following questions are sought:

- Have the original objectives been reached?
- Have the expected results been obtained?
- Is the requester completely satisfied?

Throughout the implementation process one must evaluate the effectiveness of the new measures and systems being installed. This evaluation should be based on the results obtained. Normally, a corrective measure or system is considered valid when the original objectives have been reached.

STEP TWENTY-THREE: FOLLOW-UP REPORT

A follow-up report should show the degree to which the objectives have been attained and the corrective measures to be taken, if there are any. If modifications or supplementary measures must be taken to reach the objectives, the analyst must say so in the follow-up report.

MEETINGS

During the entire BPI/WS process, meetings are crucial. The objectives of these meetings are to get information, clarify a situation, present recommendations, and make decisions for moving the project forward.

Before each meeting, the analyst should:

- prepare an agenda, i.e., the list of subjects to discuss in order of importance;
- set the date of the meeting;
- determine the place for the meeting;
- establish the beginning and ending times; and
- contact those who should attend.

The analyst should chair the meeting and make sure that:

- the participants follow the agenda;
- the timetable is respected, i.e., the time allocated for each item;

- subjects that are not pertinent are avoided; and
- all participants are able to express their opinions.

The chair may also intervene to ask leading questions or clarify a point. While the analyst can also be the meeting's secretary, it is often preferable to have someone else handle this task, especially if the analyst is the chairperson. However, minutes should be distributed only if decisions have been made, responsibilities delegated, and tasks assigned to one or more participant(s).

INTERVIEWS, REPORTS, AND DOCUMENTS

The critical components of any detailed intervention methodology are its interviews, meetings, reports, and documents. Their structure and arrangement are also key. Chapters 5, 6, 7, and 8 covered meetings, reports, and documents in comprehensive detail. The key points are summarized in the sections that follow.

INTERVIEWS

The purpose of interviews is to learn about the current situation in a department or system under study. More than one interview may be necessary to identify the problem(s) and to search for solutions that are, very often, suggested by the users themselves.

The success of a computerization work activity depends, for a good part, on the quality of the interviews with the management and the employees of the department in question. Much of the information concerning the department's activities is gathered during or following an interview. The general orientation of the project will eventually be affected by the information thus gathered.

There are three types of interviews:
- the introductory interview;
- the in-depth interview; and
- the clarification interview.
- Sometimes, all three types occur in the same interview.

◆ Preparation

The main actions for preparing for an interview are:
- identifying the goals and the information to obtain and to communicate;
- attaining information about the person being met;
- if the answers require research or calculations, sending a list of questions before the interview;

- setting the meeting at the interviewee's place of work and being there on time;
- avoiding over-preparation, and
- having all information at hand.

◆   **Role and Attitude of the Analyst During the Interview**

The analyst must favor team spirit with the interviewee; this is the best way to get all the cooperation and information needed.

The analyst will try to identify the problems with the users and will try to get them to find appropriate solutions themselves. It is easier to activate a new system that has been suggested by the users than one forced on them.

A good way to start an interview is to explain the goals of the interview and how the help and assistance of the interviewee will be used. Thereafter, give the employee the chance to explain what the job is and what the problems are. In other words, listen.

The analyst must:

- observe the facts;
- lead the interview without getting off the subject;
- be able to listen;
- take notes;
- be available; and
- be able to detect key points.

◆   **Controlling the Interview**

People should have the opportunity to speak and to express themselves, but the interview also must move in the right direction. A good way to lead the interview and to get more information is for the analyst to act as if he or she knows nothing about the subject at hand.

Encourage and help the interviewees to suggest different solutions to their problem(s) by asking the right questions. When a solution is found and retained in this way, they will be more inclined to implement it with enthusiasm when the time comes.

Always pay attention to the interviewee's mood and degree of fatigue. It is a question of noticing when to put an end to the interview, diplomatically. An analyst may always request another interview if the subject has not been covered fully.

◆ Notes

Do not write down everything the interviewee says, but take enough notes to be able to understand what is going on in the department. In other words, take enough notes to reassemble in a coherent fashion the information gathered.

These notes should be clear, legible, and brief. Review them with the interviewee for validation and to make sure the interviewee's points were understood.

Record the names and titles of the people you meet as well as the subjects discussed and the dates of the interviews.

◆ Concluding the Interview

It is important to end an interview cordially and with a note of understanding. This will establish a solid and durable relationship, indispensable to good future interviews. To this end, here is some practical advice:

- do not prolong the interview uselessly;
- end by reviewing the main points;
- thank the interviewee; and
- prepare for the possibility of asking for additional information, should it become necessary.

◆ Questions

The best way to get information during interviews is to ask questions. To conduct interviews properly, questions should be asked at the right moment and be formulated in a language that can be understood easily.

Questions that result in a "yes" or "no" answer have a tendency to shorten dialogue, depriving the analyst of complementary information. The analyst should therefore ask "open" questions that need explanation. For example: "How do you do this activity?" or "Why do you do it this way?" This type of question must be asked only one at a time, according to the rhythm of the interview, and should avoid technical, abstract, or emotional terms.

REPORTS

For the detailed intervention methodology, the following reports should be submitted:

- the initiation report;
- the objective(s) report;
- the feasibility report (at the end of the preliminary study);

- the final report; and
- the follow-up report.

Communication efficiency in any type of report depends on the following rules to communicate the correct message to the intended audience:

- use language the receiver can understand, avoiding a surfeit of technical jargon and retaining simple, everyday words;
- catch the reader's attention with the first lines of the report;
- prepare and transmit reports that reflect corporate philosophy; and
- make sure that all information transmitted to managers is as accurate as possible, correcting any misunderstandings through the formal organization.

A report should contain no surprises. Managers should be given the opportunity to read a draft before it is finalized. Always try to consult with the personnel affected before a report is published.

Each report warrants special attention. The facts presented must reflect reality. While the main weaknesses identified must be noted, this should be done in the context of an overall evaluation, not as a list of areas requiring improvement. The report must be written with a view to helping management create and implement means improving the productivity of the department.

The presentation of the report must be professional. While a polished presentation cannot hide a bad report, a poor presentation can jeopardize an excellent report. Moreover, reports have a tendency to gravitate upwards. The effort made to polish a presentation will not be wasted when it lands in the hands of senior management.

The report must be written and organized to help managers understand and accept its message.

Normally, each report should contain one or more of the following chapters, as the case may be:

- introduction:
  -identification of the subject,
  -objective(s) of the mandate,
  -approach of the study, and
  -structure of the report;
- main points:
  -global evaluation of the subject,
  -summary of important shortcomings, and
  -pertinent recommendations;

- organizational impact:
  -potential and significant impact of the recommendations;
- conclusion:
  -objectives met,
  -urgent situations,
  -department management's perception, and
  -department management's comments;
- acknowledgments; and
- appendices:
  -overview of existing activities, and
  -description of the shortcomings, consequences, and
    recommendations.

DOCUMENTS

Documents are crucial to all BPI/WS studies. They must be kept and arranged for access even after the study is complete.

◆ Filing Study Documents

It is preferable to file all documents for each study in chronological order. Start with the oldest (the original request) on the bottom. In a perfect world, this order would be:

- the request;
- the initiation report;
- the planning documents;
- the preliminary analysis documents, flow charts, etc.;
- the objective(s) report;
- the feasibility report (preliminary analysis report);
- the final report; and
- the follow-up report.

◆ Storage of Documents

Each study file should be kept in the office (or filing cabinet) of the analyst responsible for the study, while closed or follow-up files must be kept in an archive filing cabinet in the BPI/WS Department.

Files should be kept long enough to be able to follow-up on the recommendations made. Allow for an additional reasonable period to be able to answer questions from managers or senior management that could arise later on. Files should therefore be kept as long as they may be needed for reference.

CONCLUSION

In this chapter, the steps, methods, and principles laid down in preceding chapters were combined to produce a detailed intervention methodology that can be used by a BPI/WS department or analyst. The key components of a BPI/WS study were also reviewed to remind analysts and departments that they are as important as the methodology itself. If the steps and the advice set forth in this chapter are followed by a professional, well-trained BPI/WS analyst or consultant, there can be no end to what he or she can accomplish.

GLOSSARY

administrative procedures — a description of the activities a group must do.

analytical organization chart — a divisional chart with a summarized description of its functions.

brainstorming — the spontaneous contribution of ideas from all members of a group.

business process reengineering — the 1990s' term for work simplification.

centralized structure — an organization in which all units report to a head office.

chart technique — one of the three most common methods of recording facts, the use of a horizontal and vertical axis diagram with parallel lines to plot activities.

chronological progression — progress path characterized by a succession of events in time.

circular — a type of organization chart that represents a company's departments in circular segments.

continuous form — a certain number of sheets with carbon paper usually used for computer printing and word processing.

criteria of necessity — criteria vital and crucial to the implementation of a solution.

criteria of usefulness — criteria that are desirable, but not crucial, in the implementation of a solution.

criterion — a principle used to distinguish the real and the false, to judge, and to classify.

critical path method — a planning and programming system for complex projects based on the fact that only a small amount of tasks determines the time necessary to achieve a project. The sequence of those tasks constitutes the critical path.

decentralized structure — an organization in which different departments report to the management of a branch office or subsidiary.

divisional organization chart — a chart that shows the functions and the hierarchical links of a particular section.

family tree — a type of organization chart where the departments follow one another from the top to the bottom of the scale.

flow diagram — the representation in space of a process's or procedure's activities.

form — a document on which permanent data is printed.

forms analysis chart — a chart used to eliminate duplicate forms and revise others by grouping, on a single sheet, the column headings of those forms being examined.

functions guide — a summary of job descriptions as they fit in within the overall activities of a company.

Gantt chart — a chart that represents graphically the evolution of a project in comparison with its planned execution time. It is used to plan the time for each project's activities and establish, in advance, each person's or group's job in relation to the time variable.

global execution time — the result of adding each task in a critical path to the duration of the project.

graphic technique — one of the three most common methods of recording facts, the summary of a complete process using symbols and codes.

hierarchical organizations — an organization in which direction flows from above and is obeyed by each junior level.

human resources — the people a company needs to get work done.

information resources — a company's useful data and information, as well as its employees' knowledge and experience.

interveners — the starting elements of the facts, they are plotted on the horizontal axis of a chart used to record facts.

ISO 9000 — a series of quality standards developed by the International Organization for Standards.

level-based interview — an interview with a company's workers to prepare for the implementation of work simplification based on each worker's position in the company.

line authority — a system under which the authority is exercised from top to bottom.

narrative technique — one of the three most common methods of recording facts, a simple written description of the facts as they present themselves.

no carbon required (NCR) paper — ordinary paper that has been chemically treated to reproduce onto a subsequent copy.

normalized total manpower — a chart that tracks various departmental needs.

objective-based interview — an interview with a company's workers to prepare for the implementation of work simplification based on the company's overall objective.

organization and methods — the Canadian European term for work simplification.

organization chart — a graphic representation of a company's structure.

organization manual — an organization's manual that includes its policies, organizational chart, job descriptions, and normalized manpower total or authorization establishment.

organization — the way different company structures are created and relate to one another, as well as the way their functions are defined and their processes determined. When combined with methods, it designates the people who manage all aspects of the company's structure and methods.

paperwork flow chart — a flow chart that shows step-by-step realization of an activity by representing, in correct order, the different phases in the execution of a procedure and the flow of its documents.

physical resources — a company's work methods, procedure manuals and forms, office layouts, machines, and furniture.

playscript technique — a method of describing procedures in the manner of a theatrical script.

problem — a discrepancy between what is and what should be.

procedure flow chart — a chart that represents a sequence of administrative operations that aim for the same results or fulfill the same function.

process — a means used to produce certain results.

production resources — raw materials, machines, manpower, capital, and management.

productivity — a numerical comparison of output measured against all resources used.

progression by opposition — a progress path characterized by thesis, synthesis, and antithesis in succession.

progression by theme — a progress path characterized by grouping elements by category.

qualitative criteria — in a search for the solution to a problem, those criteria based on values difficult to measure, such as ease of operation and maintenance, durability, safety, and security.

quantitative criteria — in a search for a solution to a problem, those criteria based on measurable values.

quantitative progression — a progress path characterized by amounts. For example, from growing order to decreasing order; from the general to the specific, etc.

report — an instrument of communication, information, and management.

roll form — a certain number of sheets with carbon paper glued to them at one end.

scientific management — a management philosophy attributed to Frederick Winslow Taylor. Scientific management is grounded in the beliefs that 1) industrial efficiency can be increased by increasing productivity and reducing costs; 2) salary increases automatically result in increased productivity; and 3) the planning of tasks and their execution should be kept separate.

simple form — a single page or several sheets without carbon paper.

staff authority — a system under which staff gives advice in a specialized field.

sub-procedure — an element of a procedure that provides for other, possibly missing, elements.

synectics — a technique for generating ideas based on free association. Metaphors and analogies are created during interchanges between individuals in small, select groups.

system — an organized collection of physical and human elements.

time and motion study (TMS) — measuring and timing the work of employees to find the best method for doing the work.

total cost concept — all costs incurred by a solution.

work distribution chart — a chart that includes a description of each group member's tasks as well as the time allocated to each task in relation to the group's function or activities.

work simplification — the organized application of common sense to find better and easier ways of doing a job. Also known as organization and methods, business process improvement, and reengineering.

work timetable — a timetable derived from the Gantt chart that regroups the elements of a mandate into a chart with headings and a time scale indicated by parallel lines.

BIBLIOGRAPHY

Blake, Robert and Jane Mouton. 1964. *The managerial grid*. Houston, Texas: Gulf Publishing.

Beaudoin, Pierre. 1984. *La gestion par projet*. Montréal: Agence d'Arc.

Breadmore, R. G. 1976. *Organization and methods*. New York: David McCay.

Cahill, N. and G. Nephtali. 1984. *Le défi bureautique: les premiers pas*. Montréal: Agence Arc.

Cajolet-Laganiere, Hélène. 1983. *Rédaction technique*. Sherbrooke, Canada: Laganiere.

Cassar, Jean-Paul, Louis G. Garcau and Thérèse Baribeau. 1988. *La bureautique: planification, implementation, gestion*. Montreal: editions G. Vermette.

Contant, Pierre. 1972. *Principes et techniques de gestion*. Sainte-Foy, Quebec: Pierre Contant.

Deming, W. Edward. 1986. *Out of the crisis*. Cambridge, Mass.: MIT Press.

Drucker, P. F. , 1974. *Management: tasks, responsibilities, practices*. New York: Harper and Row.

Dubé, Léonard. 1980. *Organisation et structures: autonomie et coordination*. Montréal: France-Amérique.

Fayol, Henri. 1949. *General and industrial management*. New York.

Filiatrault, Pierre and Yvon-G. Perreault. 1974. *L'administateur et la prise de décision*. Montreal: editions du Jour.

Gall, John. 1975. *Systemantics*. New York: Pocket Books.

Grace, Rich. 1994. *Using Power Point 4 for Windows*. Indianapolis:

QUE Coporation.

Graham, Ben S. 1971. *Paperwork simplification.* Standard Register Company.

Graham, Ben S., Jr. Seminar notes.

—— and Parvin S. Titus, 1979. *The amazing oversight.* New York: AMACOM.

Herzberg, F. 1976. *The managerial choice: to be efficient and to be human.* Burr Ridge, Ill.: Dow-Jones Irwin.

Hogue, J.-Pierre. 1980. *l'homme et organisation.* Montréal: ed. Beauchemin.

Jackson, Clyde F. 1977. *Business writing.* Cleveland, Ohio: Association for Systems Management.

Kepner, C. H. and B. B. Tregoe. 1965. *The rational manager: a systematic approach to problem solving and decision making.* New York: McGraw-Hill.

Mathies, Leslie. 1977. *The new playscript procedure.* Stamford, Conn.: Management Tool for Action Office Publishing.

McGregor, Douglas. 1960. *The human side of enterprise.* New York: McGraw-Hill.

Mogensen, Allan. Seminar notes.

—— and Rosario Rausa. 1989. *Mogy: an autobiography.* Chesapeake, Va.: Father of Work Simplification Idea Associates.

Myers, M. Scott. 1991. *Every employee a manager: more meaningful work through job enrichment.* Third edition. New York: McGraw-Hill.

Pitre, André and Jacques Charest. 1985. *L'analyse de système: un outil de la bureautique.* Montreal: ed. Agence díArc.

Taylor, Frederick W. 1911. *The principles of scientific management.* New York: Harper and Brothers.

Tézenas, J. 1971. *Dictionnaire de l'organisation et de la gestion.* Paris: Les Èditions d'organisation.

Vough, Clair F. and Bernard Asbell. 1975. *Tapping the human resources.* New York: AMACOM.

Walton, Mary. 1986. *The Deming management method.* New York: Perigree Books.

INDEX

ABOUT THE AUTHOR

Pierre Theriault has more than 20 years of experience in work simplification and management training and development. He has led a number of seminars in the U.S. and Canada on various aspects of work simplification, reengineering, and business process improvement. He is the founder and currently serves as president of Les Conseillers en Organisation et Formation, Inc., in Montreal, Quebec.

ABOUT EMP

ENGINEERING & MANAGEMENT PRESS (EMP) is the book publishing division of the Institute of Industrial Engineers. EMP was founded in 1981 as Industrial Engineering and Management Press (IE&MP). In 1995, IE&MP was "reengineered" as ENGINEERING & MANAGEMENT PRESS by an entirely new staff.

As both IE&MP and EMP, the press has a history of publishing successful titles. Recent successes include: *Toyota Production System, 2nd Edition*; *Beyond the Basics of Reengineering*; *Business Process Reengineering: Current Issues and Applications*; and *Managing Quality in America's Most Admired Companies*.

EMP's newest titles are *Manufacturing and the Internet*; *By What Method?*; *Simulation Made Easy*; *Essential Career Skills for Engineers*, and *Design of Experiments for Process Improvement and Quality Assurance*.

For more information about EMP or to request a free catalog of EMP's current titles, please call IIE Member & Customer Service at 800-494-0460 or 770-449-0460.

ABOUT IIE

Founded in 1948, the Institute of Industrial Engineers (IIE) is comprised of more than 25,000 members throughout the U.S. and 89 other countries. IIE is the only international, nonprofit professional society dedicated to advancing the technical and managerial excellence of industrial engineers and all individuals involved in improving overall quality and productivity. IIE is committed to providing timely information about the profession to its membership, to professionals who practice industrial engineering skills, and to the general public.

IIE provides continuing education opportunities to members to keep them current on the latest technologies and systems that contribute to career advancement. The Institute provides products and services to aid in this endeavor, including professional magazines, periodicals, books, conferences and seminars.

For more information about membership in IIE, please contact IIE Member and Customer Service at 800-494-0460 or 770-449-0460.